Mar
Difficu

D1350630

658·30
w.

DUMFRIES & GALLOWAY COLLEGE

Heath

Managing Difficult People

Effective management strategies
for handling challenging behaviour

KAREN MANNERING
2nd edition

How To Books

Published by How To Books Ltd,
3 Newtec Place, Magdalen Road,
Oxford OX4 1RE, United Kingdom.
Tel: (01865) 793806. Fax: (01865) 248780.
info@howtobooks.co.uk
www.howtobooks.co.uk

First edition 2000
Second edition 2001

British Library Cataloguing in Publication Data.
A catalogue record for this book is available from
the British Library.

Edited by Alison Wilson
Cartoons by Mike Flanagan
Cover design by Shireen Nathoo Design
Cover image by PhotoDisc

Produced for How To Books by Deer Park Productions
Typeset by Kestrel Data, Exeter
Printed and bound by Cromwell Press Ltd, Trowbridge, Wiltshire

NOTE: The material contained in this book is set out in good
faith for general guidance and no liability can be accepted
for loss or expense incurred as a result of relying in particular
circumstances on statements made in the book. Laws and
regulations are complex and liable to change, and readers should
check the current position with the relevant authorities before
making personal arrangements.

Contents

List of Illustrations

Preface

People management is now considered one of the most important skills for employability in the future. Being adept at communicating and enabling others to complete work and meet targets will be the number one skill. Start working towards that now and your career will be on the path to a brilliant future.

At work and in our leisure time we are often confronted by difficult people and awkward situations, and they seem to come at us from every angle. How can we cope? People don't change easily, so is there any such thing as a 'tool box' of useful techniques to enable us to simply get the job done?

Seeing beyond the difficult behaviour and understanding why some people act in this way can help you to manage the situation. That, coupled with your own unique way of handling people, will enable you to get the most from these people.

This book will show you not only how to grapple with 'know-it-alls' and 'tackle the aggressors' but also how to deal with difficult relationships, whether they be with your manager or a member of your team.

ACKNOWLEDGEMENTS

In recognition of the hard work that has gone into writing this book, I would like to thank Derek for all his help and support. I would also like to thank all the difficult people I have met throughout my life – without them this book would not be possible.

Karen Mannering

1

Meeting Difficult People

Why is it that some people are just so difficult to get along with? In a social situation you can choose whether or not to spend time with these people, but at work you will not have that luxury. You have not only to work alongside these people, but also maintain an effective working relationship with them. You can achieve this by finding out more about them and their behaviours, whilst also accepting that your own behaviour has an important part to play.

UNDERSTANDING DIFFICULT PEOPLE

What is a difficult person? This is a complex question which involves the following factors:

- cultural differences

- geographical differences

- personality differences

- situational differences.

Understanding cultural differences

As we move towards a 'smaller world' cultural barriers need greater understanding. For example, the Indian woman you work with may appear abrupt, aloof or difficult to talk to. She may not join in social chat or share your jokes. The danger is that before long she may be labelled 'difficult to get along with'.

Or consider the French man who appears abrupt, to the point or rude. Yet in his eyes he is behaving quite normally and it is you that has the strange behaviour. Allow people their cultural differences and you will find that they are not difficult after all. You may even observe that their cultural qualities produce a more balanced team.

Recognising geographical differences

It is said that people living in the north of the UK are different from those living in the south, and a north/south divide is often referred to.

Is this really true? Each county can in fact boast its own identity, some more rural and others industrial. We often make fun of our colleagues' different accents, and this can be hurtful. Focusing on people's geographical differences is unfair, but you may need to consider it before labelling anyone 'difficult'. It could be that they just express themselves in a different way or choose unfamiliar language.

Identifying personality differences

Some people have loud, exuberant personalities whilst others are sensitive and quiet. These differences can add richness to a team, after all you don't want a team of clones. However, the differing approaches can result in conflict and each side viewing the other as 'difficult to deal with'.

Celebrate your differences by ensuring that each has a role to play in the team that reflects the strengths of their personality type.

Recognising gender differences

There is little doubt that there are gender differences demonstrated through the behaviours of at least 80% of the population. It has been scienticifally proven that men's and women's brains work in slightly different ways, with women having slightly less spatial reasoning and therefore supposedly having more difficulty with map reading!

Women are more likely to want to talk through a problem than men, and this could be a factor to bear in mind when searching for empathy. Men on the other hand are supposedly more decisive and therefore if you want a quick, firm decision, then perhaps you should approach a man. However, like all generalisations, there are many exceptions to the rule, but you may still want to consider whether the difficult behaviour is more about gender than clashing personalities.

You may also want to think through workplace culture. Some workplaces are definitely either male (such as the London finance institutions) or female (like large portions of the NHS) and this will be evident in their processes and the way in which they handle both sexes.

Understanding situational differences

People can appear difficult because of the situation they have been placed in. They may have been placed in a team they can't identify with, or moved to an area of the office they don't like. Try to understand anyone who has a genuine grievance against their situation. Dig below the surface, rather than taking their behaviour at face value.

Understanding problems with stress

Stress is endemic in the workplace, and to make things worse it can be almost invisible. What one person finds stressful another will not. One person will cry openly at the desk or scream, whilst another will become a secret drinker or suffer internal health problems such as irritable bowel syndrome.

What is evident is that when people are suffering stress, they will often act out of character. If the person with whom you work has spoken to you reasonably for several weeks and then suddenly snaps at you, it is more likely that they are suffering from stress than developing a difficult personality. Don't run away from this problem, seek them out and tell them that you know they did not mean to snap, and that they probably had something else on their mind. In many instances they will apologise, and may even open up to you with their problems. One word of caution, be careful not to take on their problems – you have enough issues dealing with your own.

Difficult people, then, are people who *consistently* seem to demonstrate bad behaviour. They are people who don't care how their behaviour affects others, and who even use it to their advantage.

READING BEHIND THE BEHAVIOUR

Why do people act like this? Probably because it is so effective, and up until now has more or less:

- fuelled their feeling of power (they can shout you down)
- enforced their feelings that being difficult is an acceptable way to communicate (has anyone ever challenged them otherwise?)

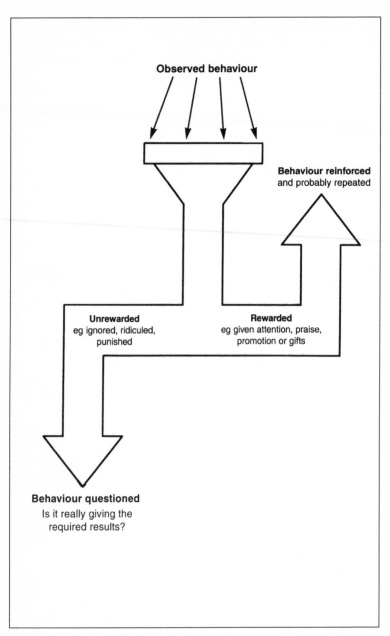

Fig. 1. Rewarded/unrewarded behaviour.

- delivered the results they want.

Are they right? Of course they are because, for them, being difficult has been so effective.

APPRECIATING WHY THIS BEHAVIOUR IS SO EFFECTIVE

Being difficult is effective because it works, but here's the catch! It only works in the short term. Long-term relationships need a greater complexity of behaviour than a simple blast or prolonged silent stance. Difficult people also hope that because of their behaviour you will either start to give priority to their wishes (because of the consequences), or that you will leave them alone. Either could be a useful strategy.

We all demonstrate our share of bad behaviour in childhood and it is here that we test out so many reactions that in time and with reinforcement become behavioural patterns. Therefore it can be interesting to reflect on whether we were given our own way as children, or whether we had to fight and argue, or were encouraged to debate. Psychologists also argue that our position within the family unit (oldest, youngest, middle child) also has some bearing on our behaviour in later life.

Whatever our family experiences it is broadly accepted that we model behaviour from the previous reactions it has provoked, and if the behaviour has never been challenged then every time it is successful, it is reinforced (see Figure 1). It is a sobering thought that every time you comply with a difficult person you are actually reinforcing their belief that it is acceptable to act in that way.

DIFFERENTIATING BETWEEN WORK AND HOME ENVIRONMENTS

We all know that difficult people are not restricted to the workplace. However, the approach we take when dealing with difficult people at work compared with difficult people in the home will be quite different. Many people know of an example where the person may be stroppy and demanding in the office, only to be totally submissive in the home. Why should this be?

The difference between the two environments lies in the more complex relationships we have in our home and with our families, and our attitudes to them. Working relationships have few emotional ties and are far more detached whereas within the home environment lurks a complex web of history and emotions. It is likely that you are more vulnerable in your own home as sensitivities are higher. Before making a request or answering someone assertively, your mind will quickly calculate what you have to lose. The stakes are much higher in upsetting the status quo at home than at work. At work you may never see that person again, at home you will not only need to live with them in close proximity, you may also rely on them to fulfil other needs (cooking, washing, gardening, friendship, *etc*).

This does not mean that you should not tackle a difficult person in your home environment, just that you should think through the approach you might take, weighing up the pros and cons carefully including your long-term relationship.

PLANNING AND PREPARATION

If you are aiming to be more effective in your interactions with difficult people, you will need to plan and prepare. In the first instance it may seem alien to you to react in the new ways suggested, but stick with it, and soon you will be measuring each difficult person against the examples found in Chapter 3 – and dealing with them accordingly.

Your first step should be to read this book thoroughly, completing the 'Action Points' at the end of each chapter. This alone will provide you with tools and techniques to try. To supplement this you may find it helpful to read other texts listed in the 'Further Reading' section at the end of this book. Other activities you may wish to consider are:

- a training course

- mentoring or coaching

- joining an action learning set.

Planning and preparation are vital, and this is explained in greater detail in the next chapter.

WINNING AND LOSING

However difficult or awkward the person, you need to remember that you are aiming for a 'win:win' situation. That is, that you deal with their behaviour effectively, maintaining the respect of both parties.

If you adopt an 'I win:you lose' stance you will automatically ensure that the other person loses face or is in danger of being humiliated.

Similarly if you adopt the 'I lose:you win' stance, you will be allowing them to walk all over you.

Finally to be in the 'I lose:you lose' situation is of no benefit to either of you. You will both feel hurt and humiliated and will find any kind of communication after this difficult.

Ensuring that a 'win:win' is achieved takes great skill but also leaves both parties feeling confident and ready to take communication further. Attaining that skill is a significant part of dealing with difficult people.

TACKLING THE SITUATION

If possible, always deal with difficult people on a one-to-one basis, however large the temptation to play to the crowd or gain a number of 'witnesses'. If you are in a public area, ask them to step into a side room or office for a moment before continuing the conversation. This will enable both of you to speak freely without the pressure of others either watching or intervening. It will also allow both parties to achieve the 'win:win' ratio whilst maintaining their own self esteem and respect. Avoid the temptation of trying to argue a difficult person down and show your superiority in front of colleagues.

Remember – this is not what managing difficult people is actually about.

Timing the interaction

Timing is also important. If at all possible speak to the person at the time of their difficult behaviour or immediately afterwards. As mentioned earlier, if you don't take swift action you are confirming and therefore reinforcing their behaviour rather than objecting to it. Trying to pick up a person on a remark they made last week or month does not work. Much of the way in which it

was said, in addition to the actual words, has been lost. You need
to act swiftly if you are to check behaviour.

Maintaining consistency

You will also need to provide a consistent message to that person
that this behaviour will not be tolerated again. Objecting one
minute and then allowing it to happen the next does not give a
consistent message and will confuse the offender. At the worst, it
may encourage them to persist with their bad behaviour, with the
resulting detrimental impact on your confidence.

Being wary of evil e-mails

E-mail is a terrific move forward in the search for faster communication. However, it is not always the most appropriate method for
communicating certain messages and therefore you need to be
wary of its use.

Using capital letters will LOOK AS THOUGH YOU ARE
SHOUTING, and it is far too easy to be abrupt such as anwering
a page-long message with 'OK'. Professional writers have
practised for many years to ensure that the mood they want to
create is transposed through their words, but even then different
readers may pick up other feelings. Imagine then the problem,
that most people will type simply what they think at the time – it
can leave huge margins for error and misinterpretation. To avoid
problems leave e-mail for the formal messages and use other
forms of communication for general comments and requests.

If you are on the receiving end of a curt e-mail and feel unsure
as to why, seek out the 'offender' and speak with them as soon as
possible. Don't let poor e-mail techniques fester in your mind as
abuse.

FEELING YOUR CONFIDENCE SOAR

Tackling difficult people head on may seem daunting at first but
after practice your confidence will soar. As soon as you prove
to yourself that you can put into practice some practical tactics to
handle these people, you will never view them in quite the same
way again.

Think back to how you felt before starting this book. You
probably felt:

- intimidated by the difficult people you work with
- sure that there must be specific ways of dealing with these people
- unsure of the techniques required.

Even though you are only at the end of the first chapter, you have taken the initial steps towards finding some answers. Difficult people are everywhere and handling their behaviour is a great skill, and as the future of more businesses lie with the people-handling skills of their staff, it is one that is worth nurturing.

CASE STUDIES

Tim is excited
Tim is 20, single, and lives at home. After leaving college and not being successful in gaining a permanent job he is about to start working within the customer services department of a large building firm. Tim is kind but has an air of efficiency about him that the interviewers liked. They know that the job is demanding and hope that Tim will work well in their small team – even though he has no previous experience. Tim sets off on his first day full of hope and promise. He needs this job to be successful so that he can gain some stability in the eyes of any future employer or bank, should he want a loan or mortgage in the future.

Christine's job is redesigned
Christine is 27 and has been a junior manager within Speedy Software, a medium-sized software company. She has worked at Speedy Software for the past five years but has just been put in the position of managing a project team for the first time. The project's objective is to produce a new piece of software as a joint venture with another company, Synchron Software. The team manager is off on long-term sick leave and the team is known to be very difficult as it has a number of 'high flyers' and volatile people involved. For this reason the management decided against allowing one of the team members to 'act up' but put Christine in as project manager instead. Christine is nervous. She knows if she does well this could open doors but she has also heard one of her friends describe the job as a 'poisoned chalice'.

Jean starts again

Jean is 40 and returning to work after raising her three children, who are now all at school. Jean has managed to get a job in a small administration team who support learning initiatives. The team is quite established but Jean is not worried about fitting in because she considers herself, although quiet, easy to get along with. Jean knows she will have a steep learning curve herself, taking on the computer system along with learning the ropes, but hopes to get plenty of support from the team – after all, the interviewer described them as, 'a bunch of ladies, mostly around your age'. What could go wrong?

ACTION POINTS

1. Think of three people who have displayed difficult behaviour in the last month. What (if anything) did their difficult behaviour have in common?

2. Using your three examples again, think through how you dealt with each. Was your treatment of them consistent? If not, why not?

3. How could you have achieved a 'win:win'?

2

Preparing Yourself

There are a number of skills that you can consider honing so that you are more equipped to deal with difficult people. At this point you may be thinking, 'Hold on, surely they are the difficult people, not me . . . so why do I need to look at my own behaviour?' The surprising answer is that often their bad behaviour feeds off your unguarded reaction. Knowing how to react will allow you to take control of the situation. For example, an appropriately prepared reaction can deflate the situation and prevent it from spiralling out of control.

CONSIDERING WHY YOU NEED TO PREPARE

Why should you need to prepare? After all, you cannot guess when a difficult person may launch themselves in your direction.

Remember – **preparation is vital**.

In the first instance you need to have a range of coping skills always at hand, and further you will be repeatedly meeting the same people who are consistently difficult to handle. If you do not prepare a strategy for the next time you meet you will always be reacting. How many times have you walked away from a sitation kicking yourself and muttering, 'I should have said such-and-such', only to find yourself thinking the same thing when it happens again? Preparing a course of actions will ensure that when you meet the problem situation again you will be able to take the appropriate approach.

Any preparation involves time and therefore you will need to consider making this investment. Time to think, time to analyse, time to read this book even. However, if you are willing to make this investment you will find that it will pay off tenfold as your relationships with difficult people improve, and it is noticed by others.

BUILDING YOUR SELF-CONFIDENCE

One of the most significant aspects of dealing with difficult people is being able to look them straight in the eye and communicate effectively. If you have low self-esteem or self-confidence this may seem difficult and will need addressing, otherwise you may have difficulty putting into place any of the techniques featured later in this book. Many of us recognise that speaking assertively to people is not easy, especially if they seem to be either criticising or trying to score points. They may even be trying to make us look foolish in front of colleagues, in which case it can take even more confidence to speak up within a group or in front of friends.

So what can you do? How can you stop yourself from being crowded out or talked down? Try looking at yourself squarely in the mirror and repeating, 'I would just like to make this point' several times out loud. How does that sound, OK? Too harsh? Try other similar phrases such as 'Please can I just make this one point' until you find a phrase that feels comfortable for you to use. Now practise daily saying your phrase in front of the mirror, believe me it will become a habit and it will surprise you by popping out of your mouth next time someone crosses you or attempts to hog the conversation.

Building self-confidence is a long but worthwhile journey, and cannot be mastered overnight. However, great strides forward may be taken by either reading this book or undertaking some training in assertiveness techniques.

Using assertiveness building techniques

Being assertive is not the same as being aggressive, pushy or bolshy. It is recognising that as a person you have wants, needs and rights. One important right is to be treated with respect, to express yourself, and to be heard. You will be seen as being assertive only if you are calm and in control of your emotions (however fast they are racing around in your head!).

Many assertiveness books are now available and they describe techniques which you can incorporate into your daily interactions with colleagues to get results. One particularly effective technique is called **broken record** whereby you repeat, in a clear, calm voice, your wants or concerns until they are recognised by the other party. For example the dialogue may go:

'I would like some pens from the stationery cupboard, please.'

'What! Do you people think I've got all day to deal with you?'

'I would just like some pens from the stationery cupboard, please.'

'I'm trying to get some work done here and no one will let me be!'

'I know how you feel, but I would just like some pens from the stationery cupboard, please.'

At this point it is likely the person will just get up and fetch the pens.

You have just shown that you have heard them and demonstrated empathy ('I know how you feel . . .'), but you have also, through repeating your message, shown that you will not rise to their bait and enter into an argument. There is nothing to be gained by their continuing, and therefore it is likely they will give in at this point.

The broken record is just one of many techniques used in assertiveness training, which can help you to get your message across whilst protecting your own feelings.

LISTENING SKILLS

Effective listening is a very important skill to cultivate when dealing with difficult people. Quite often the person being difficult is trying to convey a message. You must be able to tune in to what they are trying to tell you. If you are dealing with a difficult customer who is making a complaint, it can be quite difficult to cut through the aggression and abuse to hear their actual complaint. A common reaction to hearing this abuse would be to just switch off and stop listening. If you find yourself doing this STOP – it will only make matters worse. The customer wants someone to listen to them. They want someone to hear their story and acknowledge their feelings, and this is even before you suggest any corrective action.

Listening is very powerful. It may be that you ultimately cannot help them but allow them the courtesy of being heard. People know when they are being truly listened to and when they are not, and your inability to hear their message will make them more frustrated and they may lash out at you further.

Next time you find yourself in a listening situation see whether you:

- lose eye contact with the speaker
- constantly interrupt
- finish their sentences
- stare over their shoulder
- invite others into your conversation
- find yourself going through your shopping list while they speak
- try to complete the report on your desk whilst telling them 'I'm still listening to you'.

If you answer 'Yes' to any of the above you need to think carefully about your listening skills as they are barring your way towards effective communication.

The four key elements of good listening

The four key elements of good listening are:

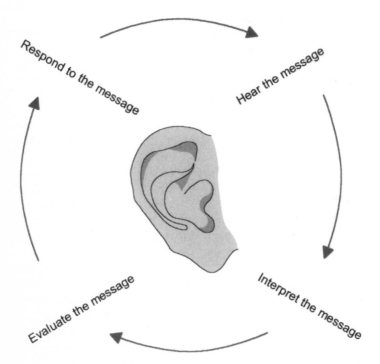

Fig. 2.   Effective listening.

1. Hear the message – genuinely listen to what is being said.
2. Interpret the message – take in all aspects of body language, tone of voice and interpret their significance.
3. Evaluate the message – decide what is the actual message being conveyed.
4. Respond to the message – give a meaningful response to the message.

LINKING BODY LANGUAGE

Listening relies not only on the ears but also on the visual messages to the brain. The brain then seeks to confirm what it has heard through body language and the tone of the person's voice, in addition to what is actually being said. Equally your body language will give signals which may be incongruent with what you are saying.

The brain is highly sensitive to body language. Mehrabian's theory about the importance of face-to-face communication identifies the following proportions as being the way in which humans transmit information:

- 7% – the actual words

- 38% – voice tone, pitch, pace, quality

- 55% – body language.

These findings have great implications for dealing with difficult people. Suddenly communication is not reacting just to *what* they are saying but also to their tone and body language – and ensuring ours is congruent or at least not in opposition.

Most of us know that when a person crosses their arms in front of their bodies, they are demonstrating a form of protection against words and/or actions. Similarly a reluctance to maintain eye contact can look as if the person is not telling the truth.

There are many examples of body language that we recognise, accept, take and use ourselves. Much of it we do unconsciously – unless we are in a difficult situation. Placed under stress, we seem suddenly more aware of both the other person's body language and our own. Next time you are interacting with colleagues:

- watch the way their bodies and facial expressions move

- see whether their body is congruent with what they are saying

- be aware of how your body is moving – is it mirroring theirs?

- notice how close you are in proximity – does this make a difference?

In other words try to gain a greater awareness of body language. Some people have inexpressive faces but the way in which they carry their body, the turn of their head, the gestures they use, collectively will give you an insight as to their mood.

Consider actors, they are masters of body language. They do more than just learn their lines, they are professional body watchers who study the whole body and how it reacts in different situations – then replay them for great effect. If they were unable to do this convincingly our inner senses would immediately 'smell a rat' and send messages to the brain telling you that the person's movements, speech and situation are incongruent. Hopefully in this instance we would simply recognise this for what it is – bad acting, but the messages could be more serious if mishandled in a work situation. Sometimes we have a higher awareness of our body language, such as when receiving a shock like being told that someone had died. The need to act appropriately dominates the mind and suddenly you are very aware of how you are standing, the turn of your head and the tone in which you answer. Body language has a huge impact on the way we socialise and communicate, so it is worth investing in some time to explore its many facets.

UNDERSTANDING THE IMPACT OF ENVIRONMENT

In dealing with difficult people the environment you choose can either aid the discussions or complicate things further. Try to take into consideration the impact of your environment in:

- how your business looks to others (*ie* its image)

- whether the environment is relaxing or not

- selecting different environments for dealing with different situations.

Giving the right image

How your office looks says something about the company and how your work area looks says something about you. If you have someone being difficult about not receiving a document and your desk is an unfathomable pile of papers you are providing the ammunition for them to say, 'How can you find anything in this place? Call yourself a professional!'

Get smart, tidy up your files and set aside a few minutes to tidy your working area every day. Keeping hoards of information is no good unless you can find it when you need it. Be honest, could you really put your hand straight on that business plan if you needed to? OK so filing is boring. To lighten things up a little keep a timer on your desk and set it for fifteen minutes – now tidy like mad. As soon as the timer goes off, stop. Now do the same tomorrow and if you continue not only will you soon have a very tidy desk, but you also may be able to access information at a faster speed, appearing far more efficient.

Using colours

Much research has been done on colour therapy and results show that cool colours (like pale greens and blues) are relaxing whilst vivid reds are stimulating. However, if you link into colour therapy at a deeper level you will find that some colours are more motivating, energising, relaxing or calming than others. This is definitely something to think about if you are:

- working with a difficult team

- running a complaints desk

- designing a telephone call centre.

All these situations would benefit from a calming coloured environment, to help the team be a little more relaxed, to relax the public, and to calm the operators.

However, you might want to create an atmosphere of stimulation where new ideas and thoughts are generated. For this you may positively choose colours such as pillar box red or lively shades of green, perhaps even using clashing colours. Fresh colour mixes such as lime green and lilac can also stimulate the senses (and the right side of the brain) into being more creative in thought, and revive flagging energy.

If you have no influence on your office colours you may still be able to influence your work area through the accessories you use. Smart coloured in-trays with co-ordinating box files can make a colour statement even against a neutral background.

Selecting the right environment

If you are able to anticipate your difficult situation or person – perhaps you have a difficult message to deliver or an appointment you know will be tense – look for an environment which will aid the situation rather than inflame. Consider the following factors:

- ensure that you have privacy (perhaps by putting a 'Do Not Disturb' note on the door)

- never use a glass-walled office otherwise you will suffer the humiliating 'goldfish-bowl' effect of being entertainment for everyone else

- select a room with a calming colour scheme (not vivid colours or a heavy pattern)

- remove any distractions and/or confidential documentation

- ensure there is sufficient seating and comforts (such as tissues).

PRACTISING YOUR SKILLS

Like all great skills, dealing with difficult people needs practice. With the right tools in place, the more you practise the easier and more effective your actions will be. Naturally this will be observed by your colleagues and their reactions will vary. If they are friendly they may want to know how you handle people so well, in which case you can point them in the right direction. However, they may themselves have been a thorn in your flesh. If this is the case, you may find that they have a grudging admiration for you. After all you are the person who plays them at their own game and will not be stamped down. You refuse to take the blame for situations that are not directly related to you, yet you still seem to smooth the waves.

Remember – you cannot always control the situation but **you can be in command of it**. This will not come overnight but with practice it is perfectly possible to gain that command in a very short time.

GIVING GREAT FEEDBACK

Giving feedback can be difficult – especially when it is personal. Giving feedback on work-related issues can be challenging but commenting on personal performance or perhaps appearance can be very tricky.

Being comfortable

The first rule of giving great feedback is to make the person feel comfortable and at ease. Choose the moment you speak to them carefully. Do not select a time when they are under great pressure, or five minutes before the end of the day. They will not hear your message if they are feeling stressed.

Choosing the right place

Do not select an area that is too open plan. Both of you need to be able to speak clearly and not be overheard. Try if at all possible to sit slightly to the side of each other. Facing one another, especially over a desk or table, is confrontational and you have the barrier of the desk/table between you making it difficult to demonstrate empathy or respond demonstratively. Use comfortable chairs and have all notes to hand so that you are both able to concentrate on the feedback rather than trying to balance precariously on inappropriate furniture, without the correct paperwork.

Keeping it positive

All feedback should be as positive as possible so that the person on the receiving end thinks that any bad messages are balanced by their positive attributes, and the conversation should always finish on a positive note, perhaps with an action plan. Ensure the conversation focuses on any business discrepancies and does not get personal or spiral into blaming others.

Setting future action

Finally ask them to think about your comments and then come back to you in a couple of days with their own action plan or thoughts for correction. This way they will own the problem, and you can meet together under less stressful circumstances and re-build the relationship (see Figure 3).

Remember – 99 per cent of all difficult feedback is not intended

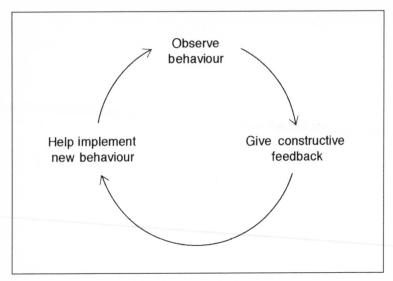

Fig. 3. Feedback loop.

to force a resignation. It is **simply to improve performance**, and it is important that this message is conveyed.

RECOGNISING YOURSELF

There is no straight division between people who are difficult and those who are not. We can all be difficult in certain situations, and probably have been! Just being human takes you part way to understanding what pressures we are all under. Combine that with the targets we need to meet, the jockeying for political positioning within organisations, and our differing range of personalities and expectations – and it becomes clear that most situations are a recipe for a conflict.

It is illuminating to reflect on our own behaviour over the years.

Think back. In what ways were you difficult and did it get you what you wanted? Reflecting back will enable you not only to empathise with those causing you distress but also to recognise some of the possible causes. This does not excuse their behaviour, but if you can recognise the cause it is possible to place it in a different context, and you will then be able to view it more objectively.

CASE STUDIES

Tim meets his first problem

Tim's job does not get off to a good start. He is shown into his new office and finds that he has to share it with an older man called Pete who has obviously been doing the job for a long time. Tim is left to settle in and familiarise himself with his surroundings. Pete ignores Tim and when Tim tries to introduce himself, Pete just sneers. Tim knew that he would have to deal with difficult customers in his job but he had envisaged working in a friendly and supportive team. Suddenly the phones start ringing and Pete is transformed into a helpful customer care officer. Tim does not know what to do.

Christine gets off to a shaky start

Christine is keen to get off on the right foot. She calls the team together on her first morning so that she can introduce herself and give them an opportunity to ask her any questions. She is annoyed when, without hesitation, one team member called Mike jokes that she won't last the course. Christine says nothing but later wishes she had come out with some clever retort. At lunchtime Sue from personnel phones to see how she is getting on, and offers her a training day on dealing with difficult people. Christine is keen but cannot get on the course for six months.

Jean settles in nicely

Jean is enjoying being back at work. The team of ladies are all approximately her age and for the first two or three weeks she learns the filing system. Jean is naturally curious about the computers on the desks but is told by the others that the systems are complicated, and that she would be better off sticking to the filing and addressing envelopes with sticky labels. Jean is keen to make a good impression and is sure that if she speaks nicely to the office manager she would show her how the computer systems work. After all they could not be more complex than her son's system at home – and she manages to use that. Jean makes a note in her diary to mention it when she sees her manager at her next month's meeting.

ACTION POINTS

1. Think about the environments available to you. Where would you take someone who you knew to be difficult? Is a better environment available?

2. Keep a log on any difficult situation you encounter. Who said what? What was the tone/body language? How did you handle it? What would you do differently next time? Write down your thoughts and re-visit them regularly.

3. Consider your own personality and the way you interact with others. Be honest, in what ways are *you* a difficult person?

3

Identifying Difficult Behaviour

There are many types of difficult people, and the most common are dealt with below. They vary from those who like to use noise to get what they want, to those who prefer to use silence. The one thing they all have in common is that their game plan has always been that this behaviour either gets them what they want or, by belittling the other person, they feel more powerful. You are not looking to change their behaviour – you probably couldn't! Your objective is to manage their behaviour so that jointly you can achieve the task in hand.

INTRODUCING SOME EXAMPLES OF DIFFICULT BEHAVIOUR

Ever come across the 'bear' in the office that everyone is frightened of approaching with more work? People are so scared of going near them that they give the work to someone else. Perhaps you know of someone who always leaves decisions unmade so that they have to be picked up by another member of staff. Or maybe a colleague consistently either does not turn up to meetings (or leaves early) so that when the actions are divided up, they get away with a very light load – after all it is unlikely that they will be given actions in their absence. Then there is the person who regularly does not deliver, but always blames others.

Why should you recognise these people? Mainly because they appear in every working situation, and also because you may have been the recipient of their deeds. Perhaps it is you who has been given the extra work they should have done, or perhaps you have been that manager, passing work on to someone else rather than tackling the issue. Whichever you are, if you tolerate this behaviour you will only perpetuate it.

TACKLING AGGRESSION

Aggression is a common form of difficult behaviour. There are three main types of aggressor:

- the steamroller
- the hostile heckler
- the temper tantrums.

Stopping the steamroller

Storming through life seems easy to the steamroller. How do you recognise them? They come at you, finger pointing directly in your face, shouting their argument or accusation and use their physical presence to intimidate you. They like it when you are sitting so that they may stand and tower over you, giving them the physical advantage. No matter their actual height (steamrollers are not necessarily tall people) they actually seem to grow when roused, and their wide gesturing movements make them appear broad too. They make decisions based on the information as they see it at that moment, and from then on have the absolute need to prove by any methods that they are right.

There are two main mechanisms for dealing with steamrollers:

1. Stand up to them – do not go silent or acquiesce as this is exactly what they want and expect you to do.
2. Avoid entering into a fight – steamrollers are very good at arguing, after all this is why they use this technique. If you argue, the likely scenario is that they will first escalate and then win the argument, leaving you feeling that they have even more power over you and feeding their ego at the cost of yours.

Stand up (physically) and look them in the eye, but without aggression or staring and say, 'I disagree with you on that point . . .'. Even better is to add a personal beginning to your sentence by saying, 'In my opinion (or in my judgement) that is not a good idea . . .'. This needs to be immediately followed up with, 'but I'd like to know more' or, 'but could you expand on that for me, Dave?'

Using the aggressor's name is very effective in making them aware of their behaviour and softening the relationship.

Aggressors like to act impersonally; bringing in a personal element, such as their name, changes the nature of the relationship.

Halting the hostile hecklers

Hostile hecklers work from behind cover – the cover being the protection afforded by other people, as in music hall days. These days they sit in the office and heckle your presentation or meeting – but always they have the cover of:

- other people

- humour (although do not confuse this with cynicism).

They seem such wits that you think they cannot possibly be aggressors but they are trying to knock you down as surely as if they had acted like the steamroller. Also their comments seem to be so appreciated by the others that it is difficult to see what harm is being done – but of course they are undermining you and your professionalism, especially in the presence of your colleagues or managers. They take a swipe at you and your ideas, and if they get away with it they will swipe again.

Imagine a scenario where you are giving a presentation on a new range of kitchware which will either secure high sales in the following year, or cause redundancies. John in the audience decides to 'assist' your presentation by calling out or muttering comic observations. The best way to deal with hostile hecklers like John is to either:

- confront them at the time by saying, 'John, you are very funny, but this is a serious subject upon which jobs rely' – acting assertively towards John and exposing him, or

- meet with John later, alone (thereby removing the smokescreen) and say, 'John, you were very funny during my presentation, but what did you really mean by your comments?'

With this second scenario, John has two options. He can either say that he did mean to make digs at you or deny it. It is likely he will deny it as hostile hecklers are not only aggressors but also cowards, hence the need for the cover of the audience. In fact his most likely ploy will be to say, 'Can't you take a joke?' or 'You're just being sensitive!' at which point you should repeat your previous statement, 'Yes, but what did you really mean?' They will again have to make an affirmation or denial. All this time they will be feeling incredibly uncomfortable as they are called to account for their actions without the cover of others.

Given a sufficiently uncomfortable situation they will think twice about repeating the process in the future.

Tackling the 'temper tantrums'

TTs appear as such nice calm people, until the trigger is pulled. A chance remark, action or observation can send them skywards in a torrent of anger and abuse, leaving you wondering what you said or did to warrant so much aggression.

TTs seem especially scary as they appear momentarily out of control – and this is true, they are.

TTs only blow up when they feel exposed, frustrated or threatened. However, if you are around at such a point then watch out! It makes no difference to them whether you are the actual trigger or not, the fact is that you are there. It is because these tantrums are so frightening that they work so well for them. The most likely response is for the recipient to:

- fall silent

- become passive

- match their fury,

none of which actually helps the situation.

The best way to cope with TTs is to look them in the eye (don't stare) and just let them wind down – which they will after their initial outburst. While you are in this stance, maintaining eye contact, listen to them. Even if you think their remarks are completely unreasonable, show them that you are listening to them.

When they finally stop (assuming they have not stormed off, in which case never follow them) they may just become silent, or in some extreme circumstances they may cry. This is the feeling of helplessness coming out; the good news is that this moves them into problem solving mode. At this point say to them, 'There seems to be some real problems here but we need to sit down and talk properly'. It is important that they feel that you are taking them seriously. If their outburst is in a public area, guide them towards more privacy by saying, 'Let's go into my office/outside'.

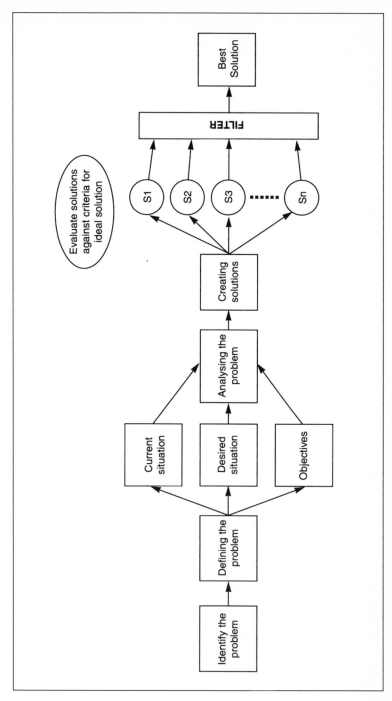

Fig. 4. Problem solving flowchart.

39

There you can get the facts of their outburst, and if possible offer some genuine level of support – even if it is only to meet with them again or to discuss a plan of action. Never offer support that you are not able to deliver – otherwise it will be thrown back at you at a later date.

Problem solving mode

Problem solving mode is when you are both working together to solve the problem. This may require you both to return to the original problem and, through in-depth questioning, peel away the issues to not only find solutions but also re-define or refine the problem.

Unless you are able to move jointly into problem solving mode, there is no way you will move any nearer in your task, that is to work together productively. Quite often people are difficult because there is a problem they feel unable to solve on their own. Their own frustration is exhibited through difficult behaviour, a scenario often played out by young children. When you work toether on the problem the load is automatically shared, but remember you are working with them not for them. Do not make the mistake of trying to solve the problem on their behalf

Problem solving is a process and is demonstrated by the diagram in Figure 4. By all means coach others through the process but they have to own the final solution for it to be implemented effectively. Working jointly towards a solution can be hugely satisfying with benefits for both of you – you may not think the other person so difficult after all.

COPING WITH KNOW-IT-ALLS

In the working environment know-it-alls are often specialists in their fields, jealously guarding their knowledge as they feel that knowledge equals power.

Know-it-alls are sometimes like the 'heavy mob' because they come in and use their technique to squash other people's ideas with their own. They simply squash other people's objections, questions or ideas with big words, fast speech, and technical jargon. They are also great at put-downs, tagging such phrases as, 'Of course everyone knows that' and 'It's only natural that we should' onto their sentences. They even give non-verbal put-downs, such as rolling their eyes heavenwards if someone dares to question them in any depth. They always think that they have *the* right answer to the problem and do not see the need to listen to a different perspective – which is seen as a personal insult.

The best way to cope with a know-it-all is to first of all hear them out. Maintain eye contact, but listen and look interested. You then need to paraphrase some of the detail back to them.

Paraphrasing is when you repeat back what the other person has said but in an abbreviated form, and in an effort to clarify the situation. For example, if someone said 'I don't know, I suppose if we raise the price of the units from £2 each to £4 each, then we might make the profit expectations required by the shareholders, but its a risky thing to do,' you could paraphrase this as, 'I see, so you are saying that to make a profit we need we would have to double the price of the units for our customers – I can see we need to think that through'. Through paraphrasing you are clarifying the message, and it gives the originator the opportunity to say, 'No I didn't mean that' or 'No you've got that wrong'. Paraphrasing will:

1. clarify the detail in your mind
2. slow the pace of the conversation down and provide you with valuable thinking time
3. ensure that they know that you have heard them.

However, you need to be careful as clumsy paraphrasing will result in alienation because it will look as though you are making fun of or copying the other person.

Paraphrasing is a useful technique to learn, especially with know-it-alls. It gives just the right level of understanding in return for their ideas. Unfortunately if know-it-alls think you have not understood them they will go back over the whole thing again, in greater detail, labouring certain points, which is often unhelpful.

Questioning them on their work is often tricky as they will become defensive and increasingly technical, perhaps steamrollering you again from a different angle. If you have any objections they are best brought to their attention as questions using the following techniques:

- **'Simple Simon'** – act the innocent. Say to them, 'I may be seeing this wrong, but wouldn't the order be better placed with Hammonds? They offered us a great discount when they delivered last month'. You may be giving them information they do not know – but always give them an easy way out of the discussion.

- **'Elastic extensions'** – stretching the future. Ask them to spin out their idea over time. Saying, 'That looks really impressive but I would like to see how that would work over the next five years, especially how it would fit into our plans to expand'. This gives you time to consider their plans and increases the amount of research they need to do. If it still looks good you can still go with their decision, but you need to know all the facts too.

TEASING OUT THE SILENT STANCE

You may think that dealing with aggressives is bad enough, and that a quieter life would be more welcome, that is until you meet those who use silence.

People who use a silent stance are difficult to assess as their silence covers many states and it is difficult to know just what they are thinking. They could be:

- sulking because they think you have singled them out

- confused and unsure what to do next

- unable to find the right words to express their feelings

- internally confused and unable to express themselves clearly

- unable to understand or hear you correctly as their other emotions block your words out

- being deliberately silent for effect.

Unfortunately because you do not know why they are being silent, it can be difficult to react in the most effective way. However, if you know that the person you are dealing with will use this silent stance then the following coping mechanism works in most cases.

Breaking the silence

Start the meeting with some light, positive chat, try to get them talking. You need to do this to establish some form of pattern, before you say what you really want to say, perhaps that you need the report they were completing for you. If they then lapse into their silent stance, the silence will appear more apparent – a contrast to their previous chat. If this happens the main technique here is not to speak. Do not fill their silence, it just lets them off the hook. All this time it is important for you to maintain eye contact and assume an eager expectant expression – as if fully expecting an answer. If you are seated, sit forwards in your chair. Maintain this position for a couple of minutes (a long time when in complete silence) and if they continue with their silence, ask them if they wish to respond, assuming the expectant position again. If this is still met with silence, you need to state the obvious, 'Pat, I thought we were having a conversation here and all I seem to be getting is silence. What's the problem?'

Keep your sentences succinct and to the point – again do not talk for them, use their own weapon of silence against them. If still no response is forthcoming then you are left with no other option but to lay the full situation on the line for them, 'Pat, I asked you for the report and you have not given it to me. I have asked you why, but you don't seem able to discuss it with me and so I am left with no other option than to report this to the project manager.'

This may suddenly result in some dialogue, or they may leave the room. If they leave you must follow through your discussion with the project manager. However, you hope they will start talking, for as long as there is discussion, you can move forward towards problem solving together.

DISTANCING CONSTANT COMPLAINERS

We have all met constant complainers. Not only are they annoying but they also take up an enormous amount of your time if you show yourself prepared to lend an ear. They usually start every dialogue with 'You know I don't usually complain but . . .'.

Constant complainers feel powerless, they feel that they can't achieve anything by themselves and want you to do it for them. They believe in fate, luck, fortune, and the power of 'the organisation' – not in the power of the individual. They complain to you hoping that you will take action on their behalf and solve their problems for them.

The technique to use is active listening. Paraphrase their sentences back to them to show that you understand what they are trying to say. Do not agree or disagree with them (this can be tricky) as it will make them continue. Don't apologise either, state the facts back as you see them and ask them if you have got that right. In doing this you are refining their thinking into defining the real problem. This way you are already into joint problem solving mode. Ask them open ended questions such as, 'When did this first happen?', 'Is it better/worse some days?', 'What would you like the result to be?'

Do not go on indefinitely as complainers love the sound of their own voice. Cut them short by saying, 'I have another appointment in ten minutes' time and need to prepare for that'.

At no point should you ever take ownership of their problem (unless it is appropriate for you to do so).

DRAWING OUT REAL FEELINGS

Often difficult people do not seem able to bring their own feelings into the discussion. They find it difficult to 'own' their behaviour, constantly blaming other elements or people for their outburst or predicaments. Helping difficult people to own their feelings will encourage them to take responsibility for them and for the consequences they incur.

The best way of helping difficult people to open up their feelings is to use 'emotional' language. When you talk to them use phrases such as 'It feels like . . .' rather than 'It is . . .' – and when in discussion try to draw their feelings out by asking, 'How do you feel about that?' rather than, 'That's it then!' This will encourage them to answer on the same emotional level. They may even be quite surprised that anyone cares what they actually feel after operating for so long on words and actions.

DEALING WITH NEGATIVISM

Negativists are not happy people. Similar to constant complainers, they are convinced they have no power over their lives and those who are in control cannot be trusted. They are sure that their view of the world is how it is, and that really they are not being negative – just honest.

The main coping method with negativists is never to argue with them. It is far more effective to acknowledge that they have a point and then finish with a positive statement. For example, if you are told, 'You don't want to go there on holiday. It always rains!' the best response would be, 'You are probably right, but I have always wanted to visit that area, and my friend who went there last year thoroughly enjoyed it'.

A negativist at work can be very draining on everyone, but rather than ignore them, try to involve them in meetings and discussions. Sometimes it helps to see the worst side of things – but never let them drag you down.

PROMOTING DECISIONS

Much of work today is about making decisions and choices, but some people just fight shy of decision-making at every turn. They sit on the fence, hoping that the decision will either be made by someone else or simply go away.

Mainly this comes from their fear of making the wrong decision, and the effects it may cause. Deep down they feel that the safest action is to procrastinate for as long as possible, although they believe that they are only acting cautiously and need the maximum amount of information before action. The most annoying thing about this type of difficult person is that they are usually immensely popular people, always helpful and willing to lend an ear to any worries. The problem is that they won't do anything about them. If you ask for a report by Monday they will tell you that it will be on your desk by Friday afternoon. Of course Friday comes and no report. Monday comes and still no report, but they are just so nice that others even make excuses for them, 'I know Bob has been really busy over the last week. I can't believe he would have forgotten.'

Coping with fence-sitters

Coping with these people includes helping them to be honest with you, which is difficult for them. They pretend to be fine when in fact they are snowed under with work, they won't speak out against an idea for fear of upsetting someone, and they don't realise how frustrating their lack of decision-making skills is for others. They like 'win:win' situations and like to see the organisation as one big happy family.

When you know you are going into a dialogue with one of these poeple, start with a positive comment about some recent work or project, or a more personal comment on their choice of clothes or style. The important point is that it is genuine. This will raise their self-esteem prior to the focal point of the discussion. If you are wanting them to appraise a piece of work for you then you can be sure they will be effusive with praise; however, before you get too excited say to them, 'Thank you so much for your positive comments, but just to show a balance, can you tell me if there are any negative comments you would make'. It is likely that they will say there is not, so press them further, 'I know you say that, and I am very flattered, but every piece of work contains some aspect, however small, that could be improved. Can you tell me if you can think of any in this piece of work?' This may then draw them out and you can be sure that anything they point out will have been niggling at the back of their mind for some time. Always finish by thanking them effusively for their comments **both positive and negative**. You need to educate them that it is quite acceptable to make negative comments that are in the interest of the final piece of work.

CASE STUDIES

Tim thinks things through

Tim decides to talk to someone else about Pete as he cannot understand his behaviour. He thought they would all be working as a team, but Pete does not want to know. Their colleague Alison works part-time only and Tim decides to confide in her, but needs to discover her relationship with Pete first. It could make matters worse if he found out later that she was a good friend of Pete's or that she did not think there was a problem. Tim thinks hard and then decides on a 'softly, softly' approach, asking Alison to share a sandwich with him at lunchtime. It is the first time he has ever consciously thought through a strategy for action. He likes this job and wants to make it work.

Christine meets her first obstacles

Christine meets her first problem. When she looks over the project plan she sees that a number of tasks do not appear to have been completed. It is not down to any one person, each member of the team has not delivered on at least one piece of work. Also she has received an e-mail from Melanie, the project administrator, informing her of a few 'hidden' problems. There is a personal relationship between two of the team members, Mike and Andrea, which can be volatile, and Alan has a drinking problem, often resulting in surly behaviour. Christine is not sure how to handle this information and begins to wonder what she has taken on.

Jean is puzzled

Jean speaks with her manager at their next meeting. She explains that she would like to use the knowledge she has gained on her son's computer to help in the office. Jean's manager, Mary, seems most keen and makes a note of it in Jean's personal file. Mary enthuses as to how this could be the answer to her prayers, as the computer work is behind schedule and with one member of the team off sick, things are not going to improve quickly. Mary tells Jean she will speak with fellow team member Janie tomorrow so that she can show her the ropes. A week goes by and Jean wonders what has happened. When she mentions it to Janie, she knows nothing about it. Jean starts to wonder whether she dreamed the conversation with Mary.

ACTION POINTS

1. Aggressives need a positive stance to deal with them effectively. Practise your approach aloud, in front of a mirror.
2. If you are having particular problems with someone, enlist a friend to help you. You can then tackle them together or provide back-up for each other.
3. Think of difficult people as difficult children. They need a firm hand and you should not let them run rings around you.

4

Dealing with Difficult Situations at Work

It is not always the people that are difficult – sometimes it is the situation. Working relationships and environments bring together a whole host of situations for which you cannot always prepare. However, one thing is certain, and that is that you will have to deal with difficult situations at some point in your career. Thinking through some strategies now could save you embarrassment later.

UNDERSTANDING WHY SITUATIONS CAN BE DIFFICULT

People are complex beings on their own, but put them together into groups of two or more, and the potential for misunderstandings multiplies alarmingly.

Add to that the complexity of the workplace. Structures are now flatter and therefore there is more autonomy, for example, decisions that would previously have been passed up the line of authority are now being taken by the workforce. The threat of redundancy looms heavily even over what were once 'job for life' careers, making even the smallest decision critical. The speed at which these decisions have to be made is ever increasing as more people want instant results. It is the battle for effective communication against the backdrop of instant information.

Bring these two factors together, people and the workplace, and it is no wonder that difficult situations occur. People often bring their home worries into the workplace too. This then adds a third, external dimension, as shown in Figure 5.

People often find a situation difficult when they feel powerless to act. Despair and frustration then creep in and the more locked into their thoughts they become, the more difficult they find it to break out.

Flexing too far

Another factor may be the increasing effects of flexible working creeping into play. While many of us love the idea of working from home or 'on the hop' working variable hours, it certainly can

48

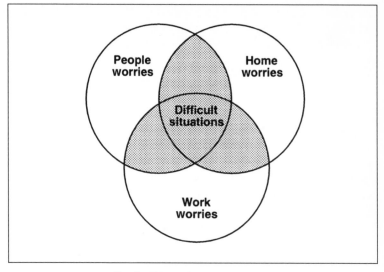

Fig. 5.   Worry interaction chart.

make home life and work life more blurred. This flexible life does not suit everyone and some people prefer the home to remain a sanctuary, totally away from the pressures and ructions of work, where one can relax and engage in family life. These people need clear boundaries around home and work, and if they are too blurred, may cause them intense pressure.

Confusing matrices

Matrix management is a relatively new phenomenon. Matrix management generally means that employees, who are working on several projects at any one time, will report to several managers (unlike the traditional system whereby each employee had one line manager who was responsible for co-ordinating all their work). Matrix management is prevalent in companies which deal in project-based work. If you are managed by more than one manager it is very important that they all have input into your appraisal. Unfortunately, poor matrix management is worse than poor line management in that, if there is no co-ordination, it can seem as if you are being pulled in several different directions and that no one has the 'grand plan' for your skills and talents. If you recognise this as your difficult situation, you can first of all be assured that this is not your fault, it is a problem of the system. If speaking with managers brings no joy (perhaps because they are too muddled themselves) approach your personnel officer or department. You need to ensure that your anxieties are noted in case of any future repercussions.

COPING WITH BEREAVEMENT

Bereavement is a subject surrounded by sensitivities which prevent open discussion. In addition, there may be a whole host of feelings, other than the actual bereavement, surrounding the person concerned – feelings which may need more specialist advice: guilt, betrayal, abandonment, fear.

Never think that you have to deal with these feelings directly. Counselling services are available that can provide specialist help and support. However, it is advisable to hold the contact details of a local counselling service – or it could be that your organisation provides or subscribes to one. You may even feel that you need support yourself. Working with a person who has recently suffered a bereavement can be taxing and stressful for you too. Simply talking it through with others can be very beneficial.

In addition to needing support to deal with their emotions, the recently bereaved need practical help. This practical help will take different forms with different people. In one case it may mean offering them a few days off to deal with matters, for others it may mean help to deal with their finances, or even with the funeral arrangements. Very able people have been known to crumble in a time of loss and therefore genuine help, offered tactfully so that there is no loss to their self-esteem, can be a great source of comfort.

MANAGING SEXUAL HARASSMENT ISSUES

Although sexual harassment is becoming more widely talked about and reported, the parameters are still not totally clear. It is not always easy to know whether an 'accidental' brush of the hand across your back constitutes sexual harassment or whether regular tactile or verbal behaviour is offensive – especially when others say, 'Oh you know Jim, he's always like that'. However, definitions do exist, and these make a helpful starting point. The European Commission Code calls sexual harassment 'unwanted conduct of a sexual nature, or other conduct based on sex affecting the dignity of men and women at work'. This can include unwanted physical, verbal or non-verbal conduct.

The Trades Union Congress takes a similar stance, defining it as 'unwanted verbal or sexual advances, sexually explicit derogatory statements or sexually discriminating remarks made by someone in the workforce which are offensive to the worker involved, which cause the worker to feel threatened, humiliated, patronised, or harassed, or which interfere with the worker's job performance, undermine job security or create a threatening or intimidating work environment'.

The key word in the two descriptions is the word 'unwanted'. If you feel that you have received attention that meets the definitions above, it can be described as sexual harassment and should be dealt with appropriately.

Dealing with sexual harassment

Sexual harassment is a form of bullying. The perpetrator is trying to unnerve you and place you on the spot. The way of dealing with this is to either face up to the person or tell another manager or colleague.

Sexual harassment often starts in a very slow and inoffensive way. The odd remark, the occasional encounter – nothing that could be openly challenged without the protagonist claiming that it was either a mistake or that you took it the wrong way. In fact many recipients of sexual harassment blame themselves for the behaviour of others – after all they allowed it to happen, didn't they?

If you feel able to challenge at the time, this can be a very effective deterrent. Simply saying 'I hope you did not intend that remark as it sounds' is often enough. Unfortunately merely ignoring them is not so effective. However, not everyone feels able to openly challenge others, especially if the culprit is some-one in authority. What is important is that you never encourage the person, and maintain a diary of every incident, however small. If a case is brought to bear then you will need every scrap of evidence. Like bullies, people who engage in sexual harassment often have a history of this type of behaviour, and it is rare that others are not aware of their activities. Your ammunition may be just what is needed to finally sort the situation out. One final point you might bear in mind is that although it is difficult to tackle, your prompt action could save some other colleague from suffering the same fate.

MANAGING APPRAISALS

Most companies now have appraisal systems. It is a time for the manager and their staff to meet on a one-to-one basis and discuss their performance. Appraisals are usually undertaken annually but may also take place twice a year, or even monthly. Appraisals are either:

- linked directly to pay and salary increases
- unrelated to pay and majoring on skills development.

Whichever system is used one thing is clear, appraisals need good documentation to ensure that an accurate record of performance is maintained. Should a company wish to reprimand an individual for poor performance, previous appraisal documentation will be studied (and even read out if it reaches an Employment Tribunal), therefore honesty and accuracy are vital.

Appraisals often contain a mixture of positive and negative feedback. The positive aspects should always be stressed first, with any negative comments fed in afterwards. After all it is likely that any regular member of staff will be performing well at least 75 per cent of the time. However, it is how you handle the comments surrounding the remaining 25 per cent that could cause concern and angst.

Whether you are giving or receiving an appraisal it is always helpful to bear in mind that most managers rarely want to lose staff. If they did then there are much quicker ways of doing it than slow death by annual appraisals. No, what they want to see is an improvement, or some additional skills developed, in certain areas. The appraisal system simply provides a structured process for ensuring you and your company continue together recognising and appreciating the same range of skills.

Coping with a poor appraisal

No one wants to receive a poor appriasal, but from time to time it happens. Whatever the reason, whether we were wrestling with other issues in our lives or had lost interest in work, the important factor to remember is that, as the old saying goes, 'today is the first day of the rest of your life'. In other words take today as the start of a new beginning. Don't skulk away or abuse your manager. Put your case clearly (whether you agree or disagree) and then demonstrate a willingness towards either solving the problem or committing to plan of improvement. Work together to set goals or targets and insist that you meet again in three months' time to review your progress.

One note of warning, if you feel you are being accused of issues or actions which are unfair or untrue, ask to stop the appraisal and state you wish to have a witness (such as a personnel professional) present. Appraisals are an opportunity to discuss performance and work issues, not an excuse to slander employees and drag up incidents from the past year, which should have been tackled when they occurred.

ACKNOWLEDGING RELATIONSHIPS

A range of relationships exists in any workplace and needs to be observed and respected accordingly. Knowing that someone will repeat what you say to their colleague or spouse may not prevent you from saying it, but will inform the way in which you phrase your words.

If you are joining a new company or organisation you may not be aware of all the internal relationships, and therefore you need to be vigilant, aware, and tread with caution. However, if you have been working in an environment for some time you will probably be quite clued up about the various connections within. Being aware of a relationship is not necessarily negative and can be used positively if you wish to convey a message via another route!

Three of the most usual relationships are:

1. friendships
2. blood relationships
3. personal relationships.

Friendships
Friendships can range from the loose and casual to the committed and strong. However, they can also be fickle and the depth of emotions involved may alter over time.

Blood relationships
Blood relationships are not uncommon at work. Often an employee will have an uncle, aunt, cousin or even closer relations working in the same company. Although these relationships

may not always have the intensity of a close friendship, they cannot be broken and generally there is a strong tie to one's family, however far 'removed'. Also in today's world of disjointed families there are many more extended family members, for example, half brothers or sisters who may not even share the same surname.

Personal relationships

Personal, romantic relationships often occur in the workplace. This may range from married couples to an 'office affair'. However, it is likely that in this relationship most couples are fiercely loyal to each other, but the relationship may be volatile or unstable.

The general rule with all relationships is be aware of the implications, but address each person as an individual.

DELIVERING DIFFICULT MESSAGES

At some time most people have to deliver a difficult message. It could be anything from speaking to someone about their slackening performance, to informing them that they were unsuccessful in a job interview. Delivering difficult messages is tough, but it can help to remember that receiving them is tougher still.

Thinking about the environment

Always take the person concerned into a private room, ensuring that it is not a glass cubicle or a room with large windows through which their reactions may be viewed by others. Offer them a chair, and sit down yourself. Towering over people is unnecessary, and pacing the floor is very distracting for the listener even if it affords you some comfort.

Communicating with confidence

After ensuring that they are comfortable, speak to them clearly and at a pace that ensures they follow your words. Do not use jargon or try to camouflage the situation by using 'clever' words. Look the other person in they eye and do not allow your gaze to wander around the room, even if they prefer to avoid your gaze.

Considering your body language

Sit forwards in your chair and look interested in the conversation, do not loll back as this appears indifferent. Use active but not overly large gestures to illustrate your point. Try to resist extreme facial expressions, for example, raising your eyes to the ceiling whilst slapping your palm to your forehead.

Closing the conversation positively

Complete the conversation on a positive note. Whatever the difficulty discussed finish with a plan of action. Do not leave the room until the other person has agreed this plan, which may be verbal or in writing. Look enthusiastic and encourage them to see this meeting as an opportunity to talk, review past practices, and take things forward, rather than as a negative action.

Finally set a date for a review and put this in both of your diaries.

UNDERSTANDING THE NEGATIVE EFFECTS OF GOOD NEWS

Giving good news is terrific for the recipient – they feel great. It can also be very satisfying for the messenger as it is always pleasing to know that you have just made someone's day. However, you need to be aware that your good news does not always have everyone leaping for joy.

Imagine that you are a senior manager and have two staff below you. One leads a small team whilst the other works as a consultant. They are on the same grade. Due to a re-shuffle in the organisation the team leader's role is expanded and the grade is raised whilst the consultant role remains the same. Naturally this is wonderful news for the team leader, but is not well received by the consultant. Also, as everyone is congratulating the team leader on their good fortune, it becomes more difficult for the consultant to express their unhappiness or discomfort without it appearing whingy, or 'sour grapes'.

Another example is when one member of the team is leaving due to another job offer. In most cases they will be delighted, but how will their team mates feel? Jealous? Pleased? Disappointed? Rejected? One thing for sure is that each person will be feeling differently, depending on how they perceived the person and the difference this will make to the team.

These examples are just two of many where one person's good fortune may have an unexpected effect on other staff.

Remember – good news is always welcome but before presenting it, think about the other characters in the equation and how they will react.

MANAGING BULLYING AND VICTIMISATION

Bullying and victimisation happen. Unfortunately one reason is that the victim allows it to happen through their lack of action. Facing up to these people may sound impossible at first but it is the only real way of dealing with them – other than distancing yourself by leaving the team, department or company.

Where there are people who have power, there will inevitably be some who abuse that privilege. It may be direct and very evident, for example, the bully may shout at the staff who fail to bring them all they demand, or it may be indirect and subversive, such as slipping in occasional put-downs until they rob people of their self confidence. They are both deadly and they are both bad behaviour.

The good news is that people who use this type of behaviour to get what they want are usually weak people, not strong as you may think. In fact they have little in the way of charm or respect for others and this is why they use the techniques they do. Now that you know this, recognise these people for what they are. Stop seeing them as all-powerful beings and instead think of them in the playground pushing and crying over a toy they want. Viewing them in this way will help you to stand up to them.

Keeping a log

If you are the victim of any type of bullying at work, keep a diary or log of times and incidents. It is also helpful if you record your feelings at the time too. This is because the written word does not always capture the nuances and tone of speech, for example, sarcasm and snide comments do not always transcribe well. If you decide to take the matter further a log of instances will not only strengthen your case but will also shock the person concerned. It is unlikely that they realised that their comments were being logged in this way.

Gaining support

Discuss any bullying behaviour with your manager and/or colleagues. You should not need to put up with this behaviour, and it may be that they are also keeping a file on this person. Ensure confidentiality before you begin speaking and ask for your manager or colleague's support in dealing with the situation. You may also want it logged on your personal file if it is having a detrimental effect on your work.

Looking after yourself

Using any support available to you. Speak to friends or a partner outside of work, or to union representatives and colleagues, inside work. You may also have access to a confidential support service.

Remember – **bullying will not stop by itself**, it is far too ingrained for that. Your self-preservation is at stake here. You need to either take a stand by confronting the issue or decide this is not the place of work for you.

CASE STUDIES

Tim finds support

Tim's thoughtful approach with Alison pays off. She is also wary of talking to anyone about Pete as although she realises he is acting unfairly, she thinks she knows why. Alison tells Tim that several people tried his job for a short time and then left. This put an additional burden on Pete, who had to carry on throughout the vacancy period. She thinks that Pete does not yet trust Tim to stay, and therefore does not think it worth forming a relationship with him. Alison asks Tim to give Pete another chance.

Christine tackles the project plan

Christine knows from the project plan that the project is not on target to meet the deadlines. She decides to hold a team meeting as she cannot assume that everyone knows how bad the situation is. She is right in her assumptions and the team are most surprised at what they hear – but individually, when approached by Christine, have a good excuse for not completing their own task. At one point Angela blames Alan for 'never being around once the pubs are open'. Alan rises to the bait and Mike weighs in as well. Christine finds that her first meeting is fast turning into a brawl. Where did she go wrong and how can she instil a team spirit?

Jean becomes assertive

Jean cannot understand her manager's behaviour as she had promised that she could train on the computer system – and seemed so enthusiastic about it. Jean decides that rather than wait until her next scheduled meeting, she will try and jog Mary's memory. A couple of minutes later Mary walks into the office. Jean has not had time to prepare but calls over cheerily to Mary, 'I have not had time to look at the new system yet, but it's on my list'. Mary smiles thinly and walks straight on. The other members of the team all stare at her. Jean wishes the ground would swallow her up; why didn't she bide her time?

ACTION POINTS

1. Reflect on the last difficult situation you were involved in at work. What were the factors that caused it to be difficult?

2. Have you ever seen anyone, or been involved yourself, in a bullying situation at work? What could you have done to help, or done differently?

3. Spend five minutes thinking about different ways you could support a colleague or member of staff through a difficult situation. What advice would you give? Do you know what support is currently available?

5

Dealing with Difficult Customers

Dealing with customers features in many people's working lives and can be both rewarding and frustrating. However, it is your skill at handling customers that will mark you out for future career success.

APPRECIATING THE CUSTOMER'S FOCUS

We are all customers of one thing or another and therefore we can identify with the role of the customer in purchasing a product or service. Most of us have all been on the receiving end of shoddy goods or services which fall wide of the mark. We have also received excellent service or goods that have not only met but surpassed our expectations. The unfortunate fact of life is that while companies hear very quickly from dissatisfied customers, it is much more rare for anyone to ring customer services to say 'Great job' or 'Loved the product'.

Customers are vital to business. Without them businesses cannot survive, and most businesses today are much more 'customer aware' and 'customer focused'. This simply means that the companies are placing the customer at the centre of their designs and processes. Customers are aware of this shift in the way that businesses are moving. Customers are also aware of a new 'customer power' they have. There is so much choice (for the customer) and competition (for businesses) these days that businesses need to forge relationships with their customers and maintain customer loyalty to their products.

As an employee in any company, your role is to be a part of that chain which maintains customer loyalty, and therefore you need to keep a customer focus to all the work you do.

Acknowledging policies

Many companies have complaints policies in operation. If your company has one, get familiar with it. It will usually guide you through how to answer and deal with complex complaints in a standard manner. If your company does not have one, then it may consider drafting one as the basis of good practice to ensure standardised treatment for all customers.

IDENTIFYING YOUR CUSTOMER BASE

Who are your customers? Your customers fall into two broad categories, internal and external.

Identifying your internal customers

Your internal customers are anyone in your company to whom you provide a service or product. This includes providing information. Therefore your manager instantly becomes your customer but so do other colleagues, for example, your contact in the accounts department or personnel section, the other departments in the company. Do they feel like customers? They should do and you need to afford them the same service and courtesy you would to an external customer.

Identifying your external customers

External customers are people and other companies you provide with a service or product outside the organisation or company, and are not just those people who buy your end product. If you were in the business of building new houses, you might not do all the work yourself and could, for example, bring in a company to plaster all the internal walls for you. In this example the plasterer's external customers would not only be the new occupants of the houses, but also the company who subcontracted the work out to them.

Identifying your customers will help you to focus your resources where they will have most impact. Maintain good working relationships with them and it will be reflected in the level of service they provide to you in return – ultimately making your job easier.

CARING FOR THE CUSTOMER

Customer care should be easy. After all we are all customers and we know how we want to be treated – so why are there so many training courses covering the subject? Probably because it is so easy to forget. How many times have you come across organisations who publicly say that they value the customer, and then do not appear to train their customer interface staff. The result is a customer who is at best cynical or confused, and at worst thinks the company has double standards or does not tell the truth.

Caring for the customer is not easy. It needs planning and thinking through so that the message pervades every area of your business. It means asking the customer what they want, and not only listening, but inviting their comments in return. Training of all staff needs to be with the focus firmly on the customer, as does any marketing initiative, sales campaign, and complaint procedure. At times of complaint you need more than ever to fall back on your record of customer care and proof of your previous good relationship, rather than shut your customer out, hoping they will go away.

Remember – it is **six times more difficult** to win back a customer you have lost than to attract a new one.

COPING WITH THE DIFFICULT CUSTOMER ON THE PHONE

Difficult customers who contact you by phone have two distinct factors in their favour, the element of surprise and the fact that they are unseen.

The fact that you do not have any prior warning of the telephone call coming acts well in their favour. Unless you are used to taking complaints phone calls all day long, it is likely that you will hear the phone ring, pick it up and **KERPOW!** – you get it right in the ear. They knock you out whilst you are off-guard and you need to think quickly to gain a grip on the situation. As in most battles the element of surprise is very effective.

Being only a voice on the end of the phone can also pose you a problem. You cannot judge the extent of the person's anger or make judgements on their state of mind as you cannot see their body language, posture, or facial expressions. It may also be that you cannot see the thing they are complaining about, for example their description of the extent of shoddy workmanship may differ from yours, when you see the actual article.

The way to counter-use these two factors is to turn them to your advantage. The fact that they may surprise you could be countered by having a couple of stock phrases ready. This will not only provide you with something to say, but will also buy you thinking time. Next time you take a complaint call try saying something like:

'If you can just hold on a moment I will get a pen and paper and then I can take some notes.'

Or 'I would just like to consult a colleague on this, please hold the line a moment'.

These phrases will provide you with a short space of time to just catch your breath and prepare your next line.

Learning from call centres

One of the fastest areas of business growth has been in the formation of call centres. Employees in call centres answer hundreds of calls each day, dealing with thousands of requests each week. In many areas, where training has been thoroughly given, the operators offer a good service and much can be learned from the way in which they handle difficult phone calls and complaints. Many work off prompt cards which help them give standard, but polite, answers to complaints. If you regularly receive complaint (or difficult) calls it might help to draw up some of these prompt cards for yourself. You can then store them by the phone and you need never be caught off-guard again.

Using other senses

Using the telephone means that you are relying predominently on speech and therefore your listening skills need to sharpen to take in tone, inflections, emphasised points, and even pauses and/or silences. This does not mean that you do not usually use these listening skills in face-to-face dialogue – it is just that, without the visual clues (non verbal communication), listening skills must be relied on more fully.

As you cannot be seen, you need to integrate and harmonise the wording you use so that the feelings you are portraying are carried in the voice. It is for this reason that trainers on telephone techniques courses teach their students to smile down the phone when issuing a greeting. It really does travel down the line. Similarly if you wish to be assertive or feel you are under attack it is helpful to actually stand up. This will project your voice further and give it much more power. It will also provide you with a feeling of (physically) standing up to the person on the other end. Using hand gestures (although not seen by the recipient) has a similar effect, especially when trying to explain a complex issue.

Using your voice effectively

Keep your voice steady and level. Complaint calls are usually delivered at quite a fast pace. This needs to be calmed down and using a steady voice yourself is a good way of achieving this. Reducing pace tends to reduce the anxiety, before the whole thing spins out of orbit!

Other rules are:

- Do not use jargon.

- Speak clearly (but do not patronise).

- Empathise with the person but at no time accept liability until the complaint has been dealt with.

- Do not give out any private details or telephone numbers of other staff (for example, 'Mr Jones? Oh yes, he's working from home today and his number there is . . .').

- Try to get the full picture, but pinpoint the actual nature of the complaint.

- Ask the complainant what they would like you to do about the problem.

- Take notes, spelling out any difficult names.

- Tell the person at the other end of the line what you are doing, and what you intend to do.

- Be clear and keep them in the picture.

COPING WITH THE DIFFICULT CUSTOMER BY LETTER

Often complaints regarding your products or services will be in written form. This is another means of communication which tends to be impersonal and one-way. Written communication needs much thought as it is essential that the words used are clear and not ambiguous (unless deliberately intended). Also written documentation has legal status and can reappear should a case go to court.

Not all the letters you receive will have the grievance set out clearly, with the required outcome highlighted. It is likely that there will be many where the details are lost in a jumble of words, accusations and even threats. Some will contain too many details, and others will be too vague, and therefore you may need more than the original letter to gain the full picture. If this is the case try sending a letter similar to that shown in Figure 6.

Getting it right

Writing letters is a very personal matter and no two people would write a letter in quite the same way, although they may be trying to say the same thing. To ensure that your letters hit the right note and win back your customers:

- Always ensure that they are polite and set the right tone.

- Write to the customer using their name, if at all possible.

- Use their 'formal' name (Dear Mr Jones), not 'Dear Bob' which is too familiar.

- Keep the letter short and to the point, but make sure it does not appear sharp.

- Structure the letter so that in the first paragraph you thank them for their correspondence, second paragraph details the problem as you see it, third paragraph states what you are going to do about it or offer, last paragraph invites them to either phone you or write back.

- Check your name, address and contact phone number are clearly shown.

- Make sure you end the letter in the correct way.

- Sign the letter yourself – do not get someone to sign it on your behalf.

- Finally if you are unsure, ask a colleague to read it for you.

Answering difficult customers by e-mail

If you receive a complaint or difficult issue by e-mail it is very tempting to dash off a reply and just press the 'send' button, but before you do STOP. E-mails may be quick and easy, and you may think that once you have sent them off the problem is dealt with, but those are two reasons for not choosing the e-mail route. As mentioned earlier, the speed of e-mails gives you the impression that you have to respond urgently – but of course you don't, you should take time to consider:

Hammonds Holdings
Bridge Street
The Square
Hastover
HA4 0LT

Miss E Pavitt
The Grove
Pickerington
Leigh
LG8 9PP

(date)

Dear Miss Pavitt

Thank you for your letter. We at Hammonds Holdings actively encourage feedback from all our customers and we are constantly striving to improve our products and services.

To enable us to deal with your complaint with increased speed it would help us if you could supply answers to the following:

1. What is the exact nature of the complaint?
2. To which product or service does this relate?
3. Are there any specific details and/or dates involved?
4. Have you spoken to us on the phone about this? If so, whom did you speak to?

Please could you also supply us with your contact details, including a phone number as we may wish to speak with you to confirm facts and inform you of progress.

You may be assured that your comments will be taken forward on our receipt of the above details.

Yours sincerely

Carole Fisher
Customer Manager

Fig. 6. Sample letter.

Lee Banner

From: l.banner@novo.com
To: s.cunningham@yellowperil.net
Sent: 14 March 2xxx
Subject: Re: Complaint

Vry sry to hear this. Will get some one 2 ring U - pls send phone number.

Cheers

L Banner

_____Original Message_____

From: s.cunningham@yellowperil.net
To: l.banner@novo.com
Sent: 14 March 2xxx
Subject: Re: Complaint

I recently ordered some goods from your company and not only was I greatly
disappointed in the way they arrived (the box was smashed and the contents damaged),
when I rang up to speak to someone about this all I could get was an 'electronic voice'
- and no one has called me back since.

This is not the kind of service I expect, hence I am sending this e-mail in desperation.

Yours

S Cunningham

Fig. 7.   Example of misuse of e-mail language.

- what is the best way for me to respond to this person (telephone, letter, e-mail response)?

- can I provide meaningful advice or should I be referring this
  on to someone else (warning! – e-mails can be passed around
  computers for days without the originator knowing and still
  the problem is not resolved)?

Lee Banner

From: l.banner@novo.com
To: s.cunningham@yellowperil.net
Cc: d.roach@novo.com
Sent: 14 March 2xxx
Subject: Re: Complaint

I am so sorry to hear of your problem. Please be assured that we will act on this information immediately. As you will see I have copied this message to Mr Roach and, in line with our complaints policy, he will be in contact with you in the next five working days to discuss this matter further. In the meantime, if you would like any further information, our Helpline is opens between 9.00 - 18.00 on 0972 01323456.

Yours faithfully

L Banner

_____Original Message_____

From: s.cunningham@yellowperil.net
To: l.banner@novo.com
Sent: 14 March 2xxx
Subject: Re: Complaint

I recently ordered some goods from your company and not only was I greatly disappointed in the way they arrived (the box was smashed and the contents damaged), when I rang up to speak to someone about this all I could get was an 'electronic voice' - and no one has called me back since.

This is not the kind of service I expect, hence I am sending this e-mail in desperation.

Yours

S Cunningham

Fig. 8. Example of good complaint handling by e-mail.

E-mail language has, in some cases, fallen into using shortened forms such as 'vry' for 'very' and using numbers for words ('2' instead of 'to'). This is similar to using slang and will not look good to a customer, it is also not easy on the eye and can be difficult to decipher, see Figure 7 (original customer complaint is at the bottom of the reply).

A lesser known fact is that e-mails are legal tender and carry as much weight as if written on your company's headed notepaper.

A hasty response could literally land you in court. In most cases you would be wise to reply to the e-mail advising that either you are referring the query onto a (named) person, or thanking them for drawing this to your attention, with a promise to reply in writing within a set number of working days, see Figure 8 (orginal customer complaint is at the bottom of the reply).

COPING WITH THE DIFFICULT CUSTOMER FACE-TO-FACE

This is often thought of as the worst way to encounter difficult customers but actually dealing face-to-face with people has some distinct advantages:

- You can break barriers through friendly physical contact (a handshake).

- You can maintain eye contact (unlike phone calls).

- There is no need for delay (as with letters).

- You can control the situation to a large extent (choose the room layout, opt for privacy, have all your files handy, offer coffee).

The important thing to remember is that, whether or not *you* think this customer has a grievance with your company, *they* think they have. And as it is *their* custom you are trying to maintain, this relationship needs to be respected by exploring the nature of their problem first, before talking it through.

Tackling the difficult customer

There are some simple techniques to bear in mind when faced with a difficult complainant:

- Try to ascertain their name early in the conversation and continue to use it throughout.

- Let them know your name and position.

- Maintain eye contact at all times and use positive listening body language (sitting forward, interested expression).

- Take them into a private room if possible (to save their blushes as well as your own).

- Allow them to outline the problem in their own words, while taking notes.

- At no time allow any bad language – it mars the issue and is unnecessary.

- Ensure a colleague is nearby in case of any threats of violence.

- Do not hesitate to call your colleague into the room if you feel either that things are getting out of hand or that the problem lies outside your responsibilty.

- Do not be bullied into resolving the problem immediately if you are unsure; however, promise a speedy response and give a day/date for settlement.

- Do not rise to any threats – at the end of the day, if the complaint is getting out of hand and the matter cannot be settled, it may be better for someone in authority or even a court to decide the outcome.

REVISING SIMPLE TECHNIQUES

The bottom line is that customers are just people like you and me. They want to be given a fair deal and treated with respect. In the previous sections there are techniques for dealing with difficult customers:

- on the phone
- by letter and e-mail
- in person.

However, there are some overarching rules which hold true when dealing with all difficult customers by whatever means:

- Always deal with difficult people immediately. The person may go away (to another company) but the problem doesn't.

- Introduce yourself and anyone sitting in with you, giving your name and job title.

- Set dates by which processes will happen or decisions will be made – and then stick to them.

- Continuous communication is vital. Stay in touch, even to tell them that there has been no progress.

- Respect a person's personal space. Do not go too close or become too tactile.

- Use their name when addressing them, it forms a bond.

- Wherever possible be open and honest.

Remember – you are trying to move the person into **problem solving mode** and the more they are involved in solving the problem, the more committed to it they are.

SPREADING THE WORD

Not everyone immediately recognises the part that customers play in the health of a business, especially if their role seems far removed from the customer. It may be that they are a secretary and sit in an office all day typing reports. In this situation it is very easy to forget that there are internal customers, people who have commissioned this work; and they may never see or be in contact with a 'real' customer.

If this is the situation where you work then you should seriously think about commissioning some training to identify the customer focus for the company. Alternatively you may wish to handle this yourself, and using team or individual briefings could be an excellent time to do this.

Competition is hot now and the customer choice is wide. You usually only have one chance to get it right – otherwise the customer goes elsewhere. It is quite simple really, customers who are impressed with service are more likely to re-purchase or recommend you to others than those who are even barely satisfied. Make sure that you never lose a customer through lack of understanding on the part of the employees. Start spreading the word about how important good customer care is and the impact it can have, before customers spread the word, bad-mouthing your company.

CASE STUDIES

Tim seems to be losing
Pete still persists in ignoring Tim and Tim is a little at a loss to know what to do. It is obvious from the way that Pete handles calls that he is very efficient and effective – he just does not recognise Tim as part of the team. Tim watches Pete with Alison and notices that he is much more friendly with her. Alison is now aware of the situation and watches Pete and Tim's reactions to each other more closely. She knows Tim is unhappy but does not want him to leave too. Alison realises that Tim's problem is actually her problem too.

Christine takes a firm approach
Christine knows that she will be judged by the team successfully meeting their targets and so she decides to take a firm line. She sends a memo to each member of the team informing them of the currrent situation of each product, the future targets or milestones they need to meet, and a clear, named accountability. Finally she states that there will be team meetings every Monday morning to discuss the progress and pick up any problems, adding an invitation for any of the team to speak with her individually if there were any issues they could not bring to the team. The approach was firm but fair, and now Christine sits back to see the effects this will have.

Jean prepares herself
Jean decides that calling out to her manager was not a good move and wishes she had spent more time on preparation. She decides to think things through slowly and, rather than rush to conclusions regarding her manager's intentions, write a list of all the reasons her manager could have for not pursuing Jean's wish to learn the new system. Jean's list is long and realistic. Now when she looks down it she realises that there is every possibility that her manager is simply too busy at the moment. Rather than make a second *faux pas*, Jean decides to think through her next move carefully, using 'what if' statements to anticipate her manager's reaction.

ACTION POINTS

1. Make a list of some key customers (both internal and external) your company deals with.

2. Consider which customers you interact with.

3. Think through your last difficult interaction with a customer. What could you have done differently?

6

Managing Difficult Staff

Few managers have the luxury of selecting their own team. Therefore even if you are a brillant judge of character and can see a difficult member of staff a mile off, you may still inherit one from a previous manager or project team. Every manager wants to run a smooth and happy department or project, but unfortunately that is not always possible. However, forewarned is prepared! Thinking through how you would deal with certain situations can ensure you are ready for action when necessary.

UNDERSTANDING THE STAFF/MANAGER RELATIONSHIP

Maintaining the correct relationship with staff is a balancing act. It is important that there is enough empathy and warmness towards staff without becoming too close. If you are reluctant to reprimand staff in case it spoils the friendship you have then you are too close and need to either think through the way you handle difficult situations, or back off from the relationship.

Managing friends

Having a personal friend within your team or department would not be unusual. Whether you were friends before you joined, or have become friends since does make a difference – perhaps not to you but to others. If the other staff know this friendship existed before you became manager they will be more accepting of it than if it develops whilst you are in that role. Close friendships are (often wrongly) viewed suspiciously. It may appear that the friend is becoming close to the manager for favours (and may be viewed as a person who always takes advantage of a situation) and that the manager cannot see it (therefore appearing to not be 'on the ball'). This does no one any favours.

Friendships usually develop because people have something in common. Perhaps you are both working mothers, or are keen cartographers, or stamp collectors, *etc*. The best way of handling this sort of friendship is to let it be known that this is why you find so much to talk about. Next time you go out to lunch, say to the team, 'I am going out to lunch with Mary. You know how nice it is to talk about our children without boring everyone else.' This will put your friendship into context with the rest of the staff.

Managing relations

If you work within a family owned business, you will need to work well with your relations. Also it is not that unusual to find family relations working in close proximity to each other. Some companies do not allow this and insist that you declare any relations upon joining the company, so that any problems may be discussed in advance of your appointment.

Some people find working with relations much easier – especially in family-run businesses. It certainly has its advantages and disadvantages.

Advantages	*Disadvantages*
You are all working towards a common goal (the wealth of the family).	You may be expected to work longer hours for no additional remuneration.
The people know you (and your faults) and so the relationship will be tailored more to you.	You may feel that you are being watched all the time. There is nowhere to hide.
It can be cosy working for people you know very well.	It can be stifling working for people you know very well.

Not all families are the same and sometimes a family 'firm' will work well, and on other occasions it will not. Unfortunately the main problem is that if there is a work dispute between two members of staff who are related it will carry over into their private lives, and vice versa.

Dealing with family relations at work needs a gentle touch. Both parties need to be reminded that work is not the place to continue family arguments. If there are any disagreements it is better to speak with both parties, stating the facts as you see them, and reminding them that they are there to fulfil a role. Maintain a joint problem-solving approach but centre the problem on the work that they need to complete or the job to be done – not on their private argument. It is important not to get embroiled in the details of their problems and never take sides. If their relationship does not heal quickly it may be that you have to separate both parties in some way, as it could become a long-term problem.

Joining management

There are times when, in looking to fill a managerial position for a team or department, one of the present members of staff is selected. Initially this can be a wonderful fillip for the staff as they realise that all their work is being noticed and recognised. However, should you be the one chosen to become the manager, you will find that this euphoria is short lived, and that when you move on to actually making decisions and/or addressing the team, an element of 'Who does she think she is?' creeps in.

To counteract this as much as possible you will need to get the team together as quickly as you can. Call an emergency team meeting and explain to them that even though you have been selected, you cannot manage the role without the support of the other members of staff – then ask them for that support, pointing out that it will not always be easy. You may even want to ask each person individually for their support, but always be open about the fact that this will not be an easy task for you. Getting them on your side and seeing things from your perspective will enable you to approach problems jointly in the future. Wading in with an 'I'm the manager here now' attitude will not.

GAINING HELP FROM THE SYSTEMS IN USE

Find out early on about the management systems you have in operation. These systems provide a framework for your decision making and in that context will help you enormously.

Find out what is available now – rather than leave it until you need to take action. Knowing about the disciplinary procedure (but naturally hoping you never have to use it) will enable you to feel more confident about dealing with staff, and will mean that you will be able to make decisions immediately without having to disappear off to find out the procedure. Just knowing the bare bones, and who to contact in an emergency, is enough initially. Similarly do not leave it until you want to recruit staff to find out the rules governing this.

Know the systems you have in place. Think through how they can help (and hinder) you. You will not be popular if you act in haste, for example, dismissing staff without following set procedures, which might then lead to a lengthy (and costly) court case later. Better to know the ground rules first, and then act within the boundaries. These systems also provide the manager with a framework upon which to base decisions, for example, if promotion can only be given after being in the job for five years, then no matter how pushy the member of staff, you would be justified in your decision to maintain their grade.

Knowing the systems will make you appear a very efficient and credible manager as you will be able to work at a faster pace, making decisions which will not have to be verified or, worse, reversed later. Following these systems will also provide quality evidence should any action result in an employment tribunal.

TALKING THE PROBLEM THROUGH

Always remember that you and your staff are there to achieve certain tasks, and that any interference in that mechanism needs to be sorted out.

In Chapter 3 you will have noticed that much of the advice for dealing with each different 'type' of difficult person is centred around coping mechanisms and moving them towards problem solving or practical solutions. You may never like that person and, being realistic, it is unlikely that either of you will change in the short term. However, you need to get the task completed. If nothing else always try to keep the channels of communication open by talking. Not speaking will not move either of you any further forward and you will both be in stalemate.

When you are trying to talk the problem through do not rise to any personal comments, keep your voice level and your emotions in check. There is a big difference between demonstrating your disappointment in someone's performance by the use of facial expressions, and blowing your top and slamming your fist on the table. The first emphasises your point effectively whereas the second makes you appear out of control.

Remember – the impression you give will be a lasting one. At some point the disagreement will be over and which impression would you want your staff to be left with?

SETTING CLEAR BOUNDARIES AND MONITORING MECHANISMS

Difficult people and situations abound, but you need to have boundaries and in-built mechanisms to handle most situations as they arise. As mentioned above, many companies have a framework of systems or policies to manage certain situations such as poor performance or malpractice. In addition to relying on these you will need to think about how you intend to measure their standards. For example, how would you justify to a court how and when the poor performance started? If it was gradual, at what point did it become noticeable enough to take action? You need to maintain written evidence to prove that you followed procedures wherever possible.

Using the appraisal system

For this reason you need to be very clear about what is acceptable and good performance, to demonstrate a contrast. Many companies today have an appraisal system. This is when a manager will have a one-to-one meeting with each member of staff to assess their performance and set targets for the coming year. Some appraisals are linked to salary rises or bonus payments, others are purely about personal development. This does not matter, the point is that they are a written record of how a member of staff is performing. This is to be the measuring mechanism. It is very important that you, as a manager, do not give mixed messages. It is not uncommon to find situations where a member of staff has been moved because they are disruptive, but has repeatedly had excellent appraisals. No one likes to put negative messages 'on the record' or in writing – but if you do not record the problem behaviour, then the court will not see any evidence to support your claim.

Remember – **be honest**, otherwise appraisal documentation could come back to haunt you.

TAKING THINGS FURTHER

If you have to take the situation far enough for it to result in the member of staff being dismissed, it may not end there. They may decide to take a case against the company on the grounds of unfair dismissal, or whatever other appropriate law they imply has been broken. This will ultimately result in the case going to an employment tribunal where all evidence on both sides will be heard and a decision made. Whatever the outcome, these cases are always testing for both sides, and can prove quite expensive. It is therefore much better if the whole situation can be avoided by:

- retaining open communication throughout

- careful management practices to ensure procedures are followed

- tidy paperwork which backs up any action.

Mediation services are now being offered as a way forward within some organisations. They are a way of using a third party specialist to explore the situation and find a mutual way forward when both parties appear to be in a stalemate position.

In mediation a third party, usually a trained councillor, will work as a facilitator with both manager and employee to move towards a solution. The overall aim of mediation is to prevent things getting out of control and ending in an employment tribunal. It is a more gentle method of exploring feelings and options, and aims to get both parties problem solving together. For these reasons it is often a lengthy process as the mediator may also be involved in attempting to re-build trust between both parties.

IDENTIFYING DIFFICULT GROUPS

Some groups of people will necessarily be more difficult than others to manage, for example where:

- there has been a previous incident and the group has taken sides

- there is identified tension (racial, sexual or other)

- there is a lack of true direction for the group

- there is a skills shortage

- there is resentment within the group

- the group has been pulled together for the wrong reasons.

If you have been put in charge of such a group it is better to acknowledge the difficulties rather than try to deny they are there.

Simply by acknowledging them you are part way towards taking corrective action. If you deny there is a problem you will never be able to take the group forward.

Once you have acknowledged the problem and as accurately as possible pinpointed the cause, you will need to advise the people concerned. Take care in the way you communicate, for example, do not say, 'You've got a problem here! What are you going to do about it?' Instead say, 'It appears we have a problem here. I would like to discuss how we can deal with this'. At all times involve everyone, even if it is the entire department.

Initiating this communication is the most challenging aspect of dealing with difficult groups of people. However, once the subject has been opened it becomes easier to refer to it again and keep it on the agenda. In the case of a racial or sexual problem you may need specialist advice or support such as that provided by the personnel department.

A positive way forward is, once you have raised the subject with the group, to involve them in a brainstorming session to suggest possible solutions.

APPRECIATING THE EFFECTS ON OTHERS

Never forget the effects difficult staff have on others. Dealing with difficult people and situations can take a considerable amount of your time and energy, which is not viewed too favourably by the rest of the team.

Other staff need your attention too and by focusing all your attention on one area you are liable to 'lose' some of your better staff. From their point of view you are rewarding difficult behaviour with attention – and you may find that as you end one difficult situation, another is just waiting to happen. It could become a never-ending circle with you in the middle trying to placate first one group, then another and back to the first. Far better to pace and share your energies, and your attention – something that parents are very good at!

GAINING BACK-UP SUPPORT

There are times when you will need support no matter how well you can cope. Support can come from various sources and some will be of more help than others. You may also need support on different levels:

- **Practical support** – there will be times when you need information. Look to your manager or a mentor to help you, and also any professional departments who can advise, for example the personnel department.

- **Legal support** – many books are available on legal matters, and your personnel department will know the baselines of employment law. Legal advice is expensive but your company may have a corporate arrangement with a legal firm or access to an advice line. In addition many professional bodies or institutes offer free legal advice.

- **Emotional support** – should be available through your manager. However, you may well prefer to approach a colleague or a mentor. It is not necessary for the other person to know all the players in the situation, and sometimes it helps if they don't as they can then give you completely impartial advice.

CASE STUDIES

Tim prepares to meet his manager
Tim does not want to leave his job. He likes Alison and the company too much, and besides this is his first job and he wants to build up a track record of continuous employment. At the end of the first month his manager Bob Green asks to see him to find out how things are going. Tim has time to think things through. First he considers telling Bob that everything is fine, but wonders if Bob is already aware of Pete's attitude. If he says nothing the situation will continue or could deteriorate further. Tim decides to tell the truth, but in a non-accusatory way. He decides to be honest and tell Bob that he likes the job, but there are one or two issues. Tim makes notes and practises his speech in front of his mirror the next morning.

Christine gets some advice
Christine meets Sue from personnel and invites her to lunch. Over lunch Sue asks how things are going. She would still like to get Christine on that course but there are no vacancies for a further

five months. Christine confides that things are not as easy as she had hoped. She mentions Mike and Angela's relationship and the fact that Melanie had told her that Alan had a drinking problem – if only the team were ordinary and not some mixed bag of problems! Sue gives Christine a valuable piece of advice. She tells her that there is nothing particularly bad about the team, just that they are individuals, and all individuals have problems. She asks Christine whether she would be worrying so much if she did not know about Mike and Angela, or Alan. Of course not – often too much information or personal knowledge can get in the way. Sue advises Christine not to dwell on the issues but to place her emphasis on achieving the tasks. She may not be able to influence the former but certainly can the latter.

Jean works out a strategy

Jean feels out of control of the situation and decides to test out some ideas on her son. He tells her that she is over-reacting, but Jean wants to get her approach right with her manager. She rehearses what she is going to say at their next meeting – and then waits. However, her plans are disrupted by her manager, Mary, announcing to the team, at their open team meeting, that Jean is to be taught the company computer system by Janie Wilkes. Mary apologies to Jean and explains that they have all been so busy lately that other issues, such as development opportunities, have slipped. Jean is again caught off-guard but smiles broadly.

ACTION POINTS

1. Think about the systems you know about in your company. Are they the ones that would benefit you most as a manager?

2. Can you think of any potentially difficult groups of people in your present working environment? What can you do to ease the situation?

3. Who would you go to for support?

7

Working with Difficult Colleagues

Difficult colleagues create added pressure because they are supposed to be supportive of you, even if they don't like you. They also may have hidden agendas but act as if you are all singing from the same hymn sheet.

UNDERSTANDING WHY COLLEAGUES CAN BE DIFFICULT

Colleagues can be difficult for a whole manner of reasons. It may be that they envy your personal qualities, such as your skills, talents, or personal life. Another possibility is that they might covet your job. Perhaps they unsuccessfully applied for your job, or perhaps your job exposes you more to senior management than theirs.

It could be that your relationship with the manager is the problem. Managers often prefer using, or confiding in, one member of the team more than another and this can lead to all sorts of problems within the colleague relationship.

Personality types can also play a part. Sometimes a colleague will demonstrate difficult behaviour because they don't fit into the team. Perhaps you are all quiet workers and they are extrovert. They may become annoyingly over-extrovert to show their frustration.

LOOKING WITHIN OURSELVES

If you are confronted with a difficult colleague, it can sometimes be useful to look to your own behaviour first. Is there any way that you could have either caused their difficult behaviour or inflamed or encouraged it? Be honest and remember it is not reasonable to label retaliation as difficult behaviour.

If you can find nothing in your own behaviour, look at the situation or environment you both work in. Have you recently been promoted or singled out for praise? Has the other person been physically moved from one desk to another? Has their work load been adjusted in any way? Remember we are not looking to excuse their behaviour, but to understand how we fit into the manner in which they are responding.

Identifying these 'triggers' can not only help to manage the current situation but also prevent the same thing happening again in the future.

Finding favours

There is a saying, 'never a lender nor a borrower be' and that is great advice. So often when we ask too many favours of colleagues we find ourselves seriously in their debt, and the same is true if they ask too much of us. What is really happening here is the scales are being tipped out of balance, and that feels uncomfortable (see Figure 9). Most people naturally like to feel some order of balance, for example each person paying for a round of drinks or taking it in turn to pay for lunch. Tipping that balance, even if you are doing so out of generosity, can feel strangely unsettling to your colleague. An example of this is often seen in lottery winners or people who become celebrities. They are convinced that they have not changed and that they would now like to treat some of their friends – after all they can now afford it, so why is it that some of their past friends seem to drift away? It is mainly because the balance has shifted, and it needs exceptional friendship and a sensitivity on both sides to cope with that.

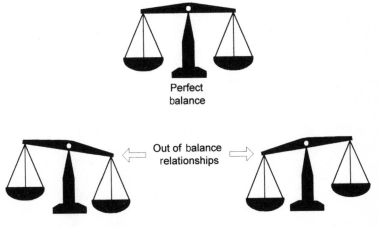

Perfect
balance

Out of balance
relationships

Fig. 9.   Balancing relationships.

HANDLING CONFLICT AND ANGER

From time to time there may be conflict and anger between colleagues. Unless kept between the parties concerned it will spill over, affecting other staff.

Conflict and anger are natural feelings but, unlike joy and happiness, when directed at a colleague can drag both of you down into a spiral of destruction, making productive work impossible.

Exposing the dilemma

Normally if placed in a stressful or distressing situation our reaction is what the psychologists call 'fight or flight'. This means that our bodies produce noradrenaline and adrenaline. Noradrenaline is responsible for our 'fight' mechanism and prepares the body to do battle. Adrenaline is responsible for the 'flight' and facilitates running away from whatever is facing us. In a work situation neither of these activities is appropriate as the resulting behaviour would not be very acceptable, for example, you could not run out of your office, or punch a colleague in the face, without risking losing your job. Therefore the body tries to suppress these feelings, and in doing so causes a whole host of other stress problems. Many people deal with their anger by engaging in sport. Being able to deal with your own anger is a very important part of managing your emotions, and is a great skill to acquire.

Understanding conflict

You cannot avoid conflict. A better approach is to try and make conflict your friend by viewing conflicting thoughts from colleagues as challenges rather than criticisms. Conflict can help us:

- break free of convention
- be more creative
- gain more satisfaction from a challenge
- test out our theories
- develop our thinking
- change ingrained thoughts.

Of course some conflict is not of positive intent and is delivered in an attempt to destroy. In this case you must remain assertive. Fortunately direct conflict is fairly transparent to others and within your company will only serve to embarrass the person delivering it. Stay calm, look concerned as if giving their comments your full attention for a few minutes, then answer in a calm, logical manner, possibly just reiterating your initial stance. People who indulge in public conflict do it to be noticed. They like to see you looking flustered – so don't. Another approach may be to tackle them away from their audience – somehow they appear 'smaller' on their own.

RECOGNISING THE RISKS

Working with difficult colleagues carries hidden risks. You will, without being aware, be judged by others not only on your own behaviour, but on that of your colleagues. Unfair? Maybe, but true. How many times have you heard someone being described as 'letting the side down'? or overheard 'I don't like Sue, she is friends with so-and-so', as if the behaviour of one person is instantly transferred to others. A long debate could ensue but the truth is that people do judge not only your own behaviour but that of those with whom you associate.

Another risk worth mentioning is that either you have to continue working with that person, or you may do again in the future. Worse still, they may even become your boss some day! All these thoughts will be subconsciously running though your head every time you need to work together. How much better then to maintain a professional relationship, with a slight distance. This is not as easy as it sounds, but is a very effective way of working, especially in the early days when personalities have not yet been confirmed.

DEALING WITH CRITICISM

Even when we know the critic is right, and we may have openly invited the comment, criticism hurts – especially when it is by a colleague. We can tell ourselves that criticism from a more experienced or senior manager is valid as they may have trodden this path before, we can dismiss criticism from less senior staff as 'they don't know what they are talking about, don't have the full picture' – but from a colleague it can hurt. It can feel as if someone with whom you share problems, often watching out for each other, has suddenly turned against you. There are then two sides to criticism, the giver and the receiver.

If you are asked to criticise a piece of work produced by a colleague you both need to set up some ground rules.

Criticising others

- keep comments focused on the behaviour you are criticsing – not on the person

- be objective and do not exaggerate

- do not apportion blame

- balance negative statements with positive ones where possible

- use 'I' statements wherever possible, not 'you' statements

- allow the other person to answer some of your concerns.

Receiving criticism

- be assertive

- do not retaliate by lashing out or gabble out excuses

- try to relax and listen fully to the comments

- try to slow your breathing so that you are in greater control

- feel free to justify your actions in a logical manner

- if your mind goes blank, ask for time to respond

- if the criticism is serious, ask for it in writing.

Remember – you have the right to ask another person not to personalise an attack. Other people have the right to criticise you but you have the right not to be humiliated or put down in front of other people.

GAINING MANAGEMENT SUPPORT

When you are dealing with a difficult colleague, management support can make the difference between coping with the situation and floundering. Managers understand that to gain productive work from staff it helps if they can form positive, supportive relationships with their colleagues. For this reason managers will often sponsor 'away days' or social events whereby colleagues can meet in a more social setting and get to know each other better.

Generally managers are also aware of the shortcomings of their staff, therefore if you think you are going to surprise your manager by your reaction to a colleague's behaviour you may be the one who is surprised. You may find that they are all too aware of the situation.

However, being aware of the situation and doing something about it are two different things and if it is action you want, then you may find that both you and your manager need equal support (and support from each other!). Managers are not magicians who can wave a magic wand and make situations different, and often there are other factors determining why that difficult person has been located to this project or transferred to your team. In other words the situation is quite complex, but your manager may have more information than they can reveal openly.

If you decide to talk to your manager about a difficult colleague:

- be prepared to state times/dates/occasions when the difficult behaviour was shown

- make a note of any repetitive behaviour

- make the direct link between the difficult behaviour and the work in hand or effect on the project

- do not exaggerate, but ask another colleague to provide supporting information if possible

- confirm with your manager what line of action they will take.

USING PEER GROUP SUPPORT

Sometimes it is not always possible to go to your manager, perhaps because his or her relationship with the difficult person is stronger than with you. Perhaps it is because the reason for your complaint is embarrassing or maybe you just want to talk through your options. Whatever the reason, peer group support is a valid alternative option.

Women are often better at peer group support than men. However, that does not mean to say that men do not indulge in peer group support – far from it. Peer group support can be either formal or informal in its structure:

- **Informal** – this is anything from asking someone out to lunch to discuss a problem with you, to popping into the pub after work. The atmosphere is informal, and there is no particular framework around your discussion.

- **Formal** – this often takes place in the form of perhaps a problem solving group or action learning set. This is where people meet to discuss problems, often using established methodologies or frameworks for their discussions.

Both types of peer support group are popular and valid in enabling you to gain the support of others to work through the problems you are facing.

Knowing the limitations

Remember the balance once again in using peer group support. Do not find yourself constantly bemoaning your state to one colleague, they will soon lose interest in you. There are a few people out there who like to listen to the problems of the world, but even though they may provide you with 'an ear' on a regular basis, you can bet you provide them with plenty of gossip. Colleagues who truly want to help you will try to work with you on an issue but beware of the limitations of shared support – baring your soul always comes with risk. True supportive colleagues are out there, but think through what level of support you are asking for before diving right in.

Exploring action learning sets

Action learning sets are made up of groups of people who meet regularly to either learn or problem solve in a supportive environment. Many sets are managed by the set members themselves but in the beginning (and particularly if you have had no experience of running these sets) it is best to invite an experienced facilitator. The facilitator will take you through the process and ensure an equal amount of participation. Action learning sets are becoming very popular with managers who are often introduced to the concept through a training programme, but continue with the set long after the programme has finished as a problem solving forum.

RECOGNISING THE POWER GAMES IN ACTION

The working environment contains a whole host of power games in action. This is because there is a lot at stake: salaries, kudos, egos, ambitions, relationships, and many other complex factors. Everyone has their own internal 'map' of how they view the world, and how they think the world views them, and they will use this 'map' as a background against which to make decisions, such as pushing forward for promotion.

It is often said that 'knowledge is power'. If someone is deliberately holding back knowledge which benefits others then they may think this gives them some sort of power over everyone else, a power that they can use to push ahead. Perhaps the reverse is true and they are feeding you too much information in the hope that you will either not understand it or be unable to comprehend such a flow.

Power stems from various factors:

- **Authority** – job titles impress people, and others will hide behind them.

- **Expertise** – knowing more than others demonstrates the power of information.

- **Charisma** – difficult to describe but everyone knows someone who has got it, and the world is often eating out of their hand.

- **Reward** – holding a budget or having the ability to grant favours.

- **Coercive** – watch out for those with the ability to dismiss you!

Just be aware of the power factors. Some colleagues will use them to try to run rings round you but simply being able to recognise them in action will help you to counter their advantages.

CASE STUDIES

Tim meets with his manager

Tim feels prepared when he meets Bob Green. He starts by telling
Bob how much he is enjoying the job, and he can see that Bob is
pleased – he did not relish the thought of another employee
leaving. Next Tim outlines the issues concerning his relationship
with Pete, ensuring he praises Pete on the way he deals with
customers. He can tell Bob understands the problem, but Bob
surprises him by turning the question onto Tim and asking him
what action he should take. Tim does not know but says he will
think about it. Bob confides that it has been an ongoing problem
which he has not dealt with. He offers Tim his support and
backing but does not seem to want to take action himself. Tim is a
bit disappointed.

Christine meets with the team

Christine meets with the team for a second time, and is most
surprised to find them all turning up. She confirms that everyone
received her memo and then moves swiftly towards checking the
targets again. Their individual projects have moved forward at a
faster pace, and she congratulates the team on this – they all look
surprised as they know their work is still not up to date. Before
the meeting ends, Christine suggests a team away day to get to
know each other better and to plan the next phase. Although
there is little response there are no adverse comments and so she
decides to put this into operation.

Jean faces more problems

Although her manager, Mary has spoken of her intention that
Jean should learn the company computer system, Janie – who is
supposed to teach Jean – has not mentioned it. Jean is not happy
and wonders how to approach this behaviour. She decides to ask
Janie for her first lesson, but Janie just replies that it is not urgent
and, furthermore, she had to wait a year before learning the
system. Jean does not understand Janie's behaviour as she only
wants to learn so that she can share the workload and help out in
the team. Jean decides to give the situation further thought.

ACTION POINTS

1. Practise managing your own anger and diffusing your aggression. It's an essential form of stress relief.

2. Reflect on the last time you were criticised by a colleague. How would you handle that if the same thing happens again tomorrow? Are there lessons you have learned?

3. What kind of power games have you seen in play? Could you have corrected any problem situation if you had been forewarned?

8

Coping with Difficult Managers

You may think that managers are there just to make your life a misery, but usually they have a tough timetable to deliver on a range of projects or income targets. They cannot do that alone and need the help of their team if they are to succeed. Ever thought of re-shaping your manager? Perhaps now it is time to give it a go.

DEFINING A DIFFICULT MANAGER

Managing people is an art, one that the manager can choose to develop, ignore or abuse. Unfortunately some managers choose the latter two and therefore miss out on a rewarding relationship with their staff.

There are many examples of 'aggressors' in senior management. It seems that they have steamrollered not only their staff, but also the organisation into submission! One thing they will all have in common is that they have delivered to their specified targets, but at what cost?

Fortunately the tide is turning. It is being recognised that employers cannot continue to lose staff, and their skills, through behavioural problems. Also there has been an increase in the number of staff raising cases of harassment and bullying against their manager or employer. It is not only the level of compensation that is an issue – companies cannot afford this type of bad publicity. Advertising campaigns cost thousands and sometimes millions of pounds – and this can be wiped out in one, very public, court case.

A difficult manager, then, is one who uses any of the poor behaviours described in Chapter 3 as part of their management style.

RECOGNISING THE RISKS INVOLVED

Confronting your manager is not always easy and it is best to consider the possible risks before embarking on a session of lively feedback!

People usually make it fairly clear whether they are inviting feedback comments or not. However, you will need to show caution even with those who openly state they do. Quite often these people will only want to hear praise and will not accept that there is an alternative. Saying that you invite comment does not mean that you will like the message. Of course, all this is heightened if you are dealing with your manager. It will be your manager who will be writing your appraisal or performance report, your manager who will govern any pay increase you may receive, and that same manager who will discuss your promotional prospects with senior management. Do you still feel able to stand up to your manager? The answer is that you must but there are a number of 'tricks' you can use to get the message over to them effectively.

THINKING IT THROUGH IN AN APPROPRIATE SETTING

Never decide to tackle your manager 'off the cuff'. Always think it through and plan the conversation as much as possible. Naturally there will be times when you just long to tell him or her what you really think of their behaviour, but try to let it go. Comments spat out in the heat of the moment will not be taken seriously by them. Target your comments more carefully, catching them out of their natural rhythm – they will take more notice and the comment will have a greater lasting effect.

Thinking it through

As mentioned earlier, it is important that you do not spring a surprise on your manager. You will need to be measured in your approach and that will take some planning. Start by writing down the points you wish to raise on separate slips of paper – one point on each slip. When you think you have all the points down, try to assemble the slips of paper in the most logical sequence, all the time thinking through how you are going to link them together. Start to question some of the issues, are they really the same issue but just different instances? For example, omitting to tell you about a new project, not passing on a report to you and brushing

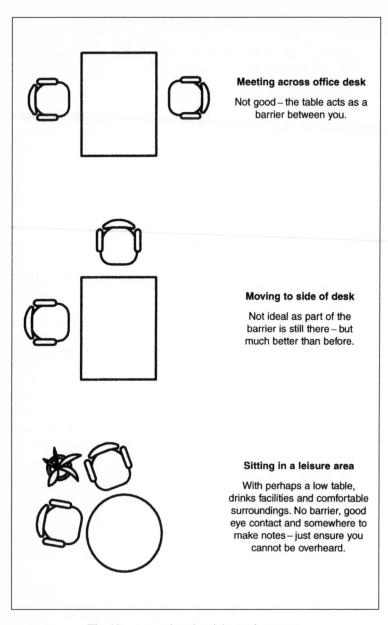

Meeting across office desk

Not good – the table acts as a barrier between you.

Moving to side of desk

Not ideal as part of the barrier is still there – but much better than before.

Sitting in a leisure area

With perhaps a low table, drinks facilities and comfortable surroundings. No barrier, good eye contact and somewhere to make notes – just ensure you cannot be overheard.

Fig. 10. Arranging the right environment.

over your remarks in a meeting are really all indications of one issue – poor communication.

When you have the real issues (with the example behaviours) see again if you have them in the right order, and then try to think through a conversation with your manager whereby you can:

- summarise why you have called the meeting

- point to the issues on the table

- discuss each issue using your examples

- discuss possible ways forward.

Finally establish your success criteria and compromise position. That is, from your viewpoint, what is the desirable outcome of the meeting and what would be an acceptable outcome.

Setting up the situation

This preparation needs to extend to the environment. You will need to get their attention and this cannot be at their desk, during office hours when you could be interrupted and the conversation never completed. Choose a time when you know this will not happen even if it is after core hours.

Ask them to meet you in a relaxed lounge area or room where you will both feel free to talk – because this is not about getting one back on your boss, but trying to work out how you can work together more effectively.

Beware! If your complaint against your manager is of a bullying or harassment nature, do not leave yourself open to increased assault – avoid being alone with them. Always ensure a colleague is waiting outside the door, just in case you need them.

MEETING WITH YOUR MANAGER

Meeting with your manager should not be as daunting as you perhaps expect. Much can be improved through your choice of meeting environment (see Figure 10). The main thing to remember throughout is that you and your manager need to work together in a relationship in which you both feel comfortable. You should be working together and not at each other's throats, or with one of you sulking or not conversing.

Although this may seem difficult, start the conversation by

stating clearly why you wish to have this discussion, something like, 'I am really pleased that you managed to make time to fit this meeting into your diary because I think we need to talk about the way we work together'.

Be prepared for your manager to react in a number of ways. They may be:

1. surprised – as they thought there was no problem
2. angry – at either your approach, their fear at being confronted, *etc*
3. relieved – at the opportunity to talk.

However, once you have started, your earlier preparation will pay off. You need to work together in the future and discussing the right way to take this forward will make for a more effective working relationship.

Using softer language

Take care in your use of language. The right choice of words can defuse an awkward situation in addition to conveying the message more clearly.

One way of softening the message, without losing its impact, is to choose the right words. Not always easy especially if you are in a stressful situation. This is where the preparation comes in. Practising with a friend or colleague can really help you to get it right on the day. Choice of words is so important, as in the following examples:

'When I look into your face, time stands still.'

'You have a face that would stop a clock!'

(section II – *The Business of Listening*)

Which one would you use?

Using emotional language can often be more effective too. Use words such as 'it feels' rather than 'it is'. No one else can own your feelings and even if your manager tells you that 'It wasn't like that', you are entitled to express that it felt like that to you. Also temper accusatory remarks or 'blame' phrases such as, 'You made me . . .' – use instead 'When you asked me to . . . I felt'.

Using emotional but controlled language will ensure that your message will hold more power whilst cutting out blame will enable your both to move forward.

Remember – softening your language is not about diluting the message, but targeting it more effectively and ensuring it is understood.

BEING PREPARED FOR REPETITIVE BEHAVIOUR

At this point you have spoken with your manager and agreed a way forward, so everything is fine – or is it? Didn't she just make a snide remark to you in the meeting that just ended? But you thought you had sorted all that out. Be prepared for repetitive behaviour.

Changing behaviour is not easy as anyone will tell you who has tried to stop biting their nails or smoking. Acknowledging that you behave in that way, and the effects it can have, is only the first step. The new behaviour needs to become established and it is quite easy, especially at times of stress, to revert to previous behaviour. The key here is in reminding them of your agreement. If you allow small comments to go unchecked, they will do it again, and then before you know it you will be back where you started. It is far easier to check small mistakes than to have to return to the original message.

TAKING THINGS HIGHER

There are times when you may need to take the behaviour of your manager to their line manager or to personnel. If this is the case then it pays to be very clear about timings and situations. If you are making a formal complaint it is not sufficient to state that occasionally someone makes you feel uncomfortable. You must be able to state when things were said, in what context, what was actually said, the tone used, and any physical implications, for example thumping the table, bringing their face close to yours, or touching you.

There is no doubt that if you want this behaviour stopped then you will have to approach a higher level in the company, where a different level of power may be exerted. It is often the case that companies collect dossiers on people with behavioural problems and need information such as yours for them to take action. Companies often make mistakes when recruiting staff at any level. Unfortunately by the time the behaviour emerges the manager is past the probation period and is well established. Further, as long as staff are willing to put up with this behaviour, senior management or personnel cannot act to remove the manager. In making a stand you can be helping others in addition to yourself.

GAINING SUPPORT

The personnel department is there to help support you as a member of staff. Check out what level of support is available in your company or business. Many now offer access to a confidential counselling service, or private talks with a personnel officer. There may also be training aimed specifically at dealing with difficult people.

Another area which is gaining in popularity, predominantly in large organisations, is the introduction of 360° feedback. This is often in the form of a confidential questionnaire given to:

- the manager themselves
- their line manager (above)
- their colleagues (at a similar level)
- their staff (below).

The results together give a round (360°) feedback on the person, bringing together everyone's perceptions of them and the way they work and then comparing it with their own. The results can be enlightening for the manager as they begin to see how others see them, and may in itself induce a change of behaviour. The results will also support any prior discussions they may have undertaken regarding their behaviour, highlighting both positive and negative comments. For the 360° feedback to be complete it requires the manager to complete an action plan for taking any development needs further.

GETTING OUT

It may seem the ultimate cop-out but if you cannot work with your manager, you may have to consider leaving. That of course could mean leaving the company or just the department, depending on how large the company is and what opportunities are open for you.

Never feel so trapped that there is nowhere else for you to

go. Many difficult managers are fond of telling their staff that they could not get jobs anywhere else. They chip away at their self-confidence until the staff believe it themselves. It then often starts to become a health issue with the member of staff feeling ill with worry. At this point it is easy to feel that all managers are the same – but of course they are not. Leaving does not constitute weakness, only strong people are able to walk away.

CASE STUDIES

Tim finds an answer
Tim decides to take a short walk to the library in his lunch time. He is flicking through the 'management' section when he sees a book on dealing with difficult people. He immediately starts thumbing through the pages, and as he does so an idea comes into his mind. Eagerly Tim borrows the book together with one on team skills.

Christine runs a team day
Christine books the team out of the office for the day and organises a facilitator to take them through some team games. During the second part of the day, she gets the team to think about how they are going to take the second phase of the project forward, and how they can communicate with each other more effectively. The team initially seem nervous but by the end of the day are more relaxed and seem friendlier towards each other. On the way home Alan mentions to Christine that he never knew that Mike's joking hid his anxiety, and that Melanie attended the same school as he once did. The whole day seemed to have brought the team closer together as human beings.

Jean's troubles grow
Jean is upset to overhear Janie talking about her to the other members of the team. She is particularly upset because Janie's tone and words suggest that she is trying to disrupt the team by securing some plum jobs. Jean does not know what to do. She thinks that the team are laughing at her, although she heard Susan stand up in her defence. Should she tell her manager or not? It could all lead to further trouble.

ACTION POINTS

1. Keep language simple and neither blaming (it's you!) nor apologetic (it's me!).

2. The object is that you need to work with your manager – not marry them! You do not need to build a wonderful loving relationship, you need to have enough respect for each other to get the job done.

3. Support is never very far away, you do not need to suffer in silence and there is always the ultimate option of moving on.

9

Handling Difficult Teams

Much has been written about what constitutes a team. Most of the definitions have been complementary and similar in context. The teams referred to in this chapter are best defined by Harris (1986) as 'a workgroup or unit with a common purpose through which members develop mutual relationships for the achievement of goals/tasks'. The emphasis on shared purpose is what differentiates a team from a group of people merely working together.

OUTLINING THE BASICS ON TEAMS

There are different types of organisational or in-company teams. Four of them are detailed below:

1. **Strategic management teams** – these teams work together to form the strategy for the company or business. They are responsible for setting the culture and balancing the business in context with the external factors such as the economical and political situation, and to steer the forecasts and expansion of the business. These teams need to meet regularly, although face-to-face meetings are not always used. Teleconferencing is increasingly being used to keep strategic management teams communicating, especially when the team members are situated in different countries.
2. **Management teams** – these teams may be led by heads of units or supervisors and are fairly stable in their membership. Their focus is more operational, and high on their agenda is making the strategy happen by putting systems and actions into place at an operational level. They enable the company to respond to problems and issues by using a group approach.
3. **Project teams** – these teams are like task forces and are usually assembled for a limited period to either solve a specific problem or tackle a particular issue. Project teams are usually responsible for the whole process which means that they will

plan, implement and evaluate the entire project. It may even mean creating marketing strategies or finance plans. It is for this reason that project teams need to include people who can cover many skills. Project teams are not always located together and their management requires specialist skills to deal with this fact.

4. **Working teams** – working teams assemble for short-term combined brainpower and can be used to work through a particular issue, solve a problem, or produce creative ideas. Often the person bringing the team together will invite the members, and they will represent the people whom he/she hopes will provide the right level of input.

UNDERSTANDING THE EFFECTS OF A DIFFICULT TEAM MEMBER

Many books are available on team building, and the focus of these is the balance in the relationships between team members. As a manager of a team, you are there to set the tone and to create that balance, and this includes tackling any difficult team members who threaten the overall harmony. The ability of the team to interact and relate well to one another has a considerable impact on the team's outputs and their capacity to work productively.

There is no doubt that having a difficult personality within a team will affect team performance, and the way you handle the situation will be watched by all. The extent or level of the behaviour is also important. If the person concerned is an aggressor there is a big difference between being too forceful during meetings, which may require you to have a word with them, and bullying other team members which is far more serious and may mean you have to eject them from the team.

The biggest mistake a team manager can make when dealing with a difficult team member is to concentrate all their efforts on the problem behaviour and omit to notice the effects on the remainder of the team. Replacing a difficult team member (however welcome that may be) will require the team to reform and adjust. Similarly if bullying is taking place then the remaining team will need support to see them through this period too. Also it can appear to other, more compliant, team members that the troublemaker is getting all the attention. However, ignoring the troublemaker will not make them stop. They are not craving your attention, that is just the by-product of your having to deal with them exclusively. Perversely they are often using these tactics to try and get tasks completed, which of course is the goal of the whole team, but not at the expense of each other.

Dealing with some types of difficult team members is shown in Figure 11.

Naturally those with difficult problems or situations such as bereavement will need time and space to come to terms with their changing life, and often being in a team can help this as the team bonding can extend into other facets of life.

Remember – **not everyone is suited to being a team player**. This does not mean that they are not effective in their work, but just that they feel more comfortable working in another way.

COMPETING WITH OTHERS

Team members are not always as collaborative as you may hope, in fact on occasions they may be the opposite. Working with others can spark sharp competition especially if there are several team members working in a similar role, or who have similar skills.

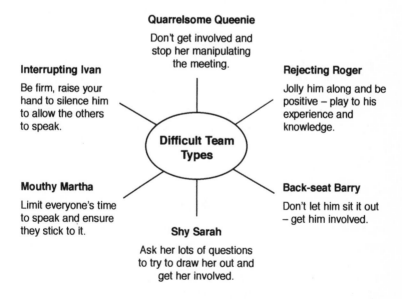

Fig. 11.   Difficult team types.

Some element of competition is good and will sharpen everyone's thinking. However, fierce competition can develop and that is in no one's interest. When competition reaches this level you could argue that the job in hand and the team targets are taking second place to team members trying to out-smart one another. Fierce competition affects not only the players, but also the rest of the team who have half an interest in seeing who 'wins' each point, but can also become irritated by others playing their own games while the team work is at stake.

Identifying adverse competitiveness

Adverse competitiveness is often seen in team meetings. Two team members try and out-speak each other, or they may get into a wrangle concerning a technical point which they are both qualified to answer, each one deliberately exposing more of his/her knowledge each time.

They may also compete against each other in presentations, hogging the floor for as long as possible rather than devising a way in which they can both input at a reasonable level to provide an entertaining result. Or they may even be in the audience of another person's presentation, trying to make their questions increasingly technical or complex, but perhaps adding little to the presentation.

As a manager of a team you will need to be aware of healthy competition turning into destructive competition. If you see this happening in your team – act fast. If possible separate the work so that each player has a discrete role and that neither role overlaps. Give them each distinct targets to achieve and do not ask them to work collaboratively with each other. You may find that, in working this way, they will come together socially if they have similar skills, and there they may even discuss their work and co-operate. However, keep their work targets separate.

DEALING WITH DIFFICULT PAIRINGS

Teams rely on relationships and sometimes collaborative partnerships and friendships will form within teams. Mostly these are positive and many people have made long-term friends while working within a team. However, there are occasions when people form pairs for less positive reasons. It may be the case of one dominant person, who possibly has the worst behaviour, backed up by the weaker partner, who takes every opportunity to justify and back up that behaviour.

For the dominant member in this pairing, the situation provides some justification for their behaviour and also a feeling of power both over the other members of the team (strength in numbers) and the weaker person. For the weak member, clinging to the dominant member will give them a form of identity and allow them to take the liberties they would like, if they were stronger, without taking any of the actual blame for this behaviour. In other words all the mischief without the risk of being caught and facing the consequences alone.

Difficult people will always find ways of justifying their behaviour and if another person is willing to back that up, they will not only welcome it but run with it, hiding behind them where possible. If you see this happening, and you wish to maintain the team in its membership, split the pair as much as possible, and at the same time encourage them to mix and work with others.

Remember – **never let a mischievous pairing jeopardise the success of the team**. In this context divide and rule is the most appropriate form of action.

Dealing with personal relationships
There will be times when personal relationships form within teams. Try not to view these as problematic. Some companies will actively try to separate staff who form relationships whilst working together. This practice is now becoming a contentious issue as the Human Rights Act is tested more fully in the courts. Deal with each person on an individual basis and only intervene if the situation is affecting work or having an adverse effect on other team members, although it helps to be aware of the situation.

SETTING A TEAM AGENDA

Teams need to set an agenda not only about what the task is but also how they are going to work together.

Using goals
We have already mentioned team goals and targets. It is important for the monitoring aspect of team management to set goals and/or targets so that you can measure progress. However,

in addition to the team goals/targets team members will also need their own goals and targets, mapping their work and outputs against that of the team progress. Doing this will enable them (and you) to:

- have a clear map of (individual) progress
- see where the critical pieces of work lie and who should be tasked with completing them
- see how their work will contribute towards the plan.

Using roles
In some teams, especially project teams, each team member will take on a specific role or number of roles, for example that of progress monitor, project plan evaluator and marketing expert.

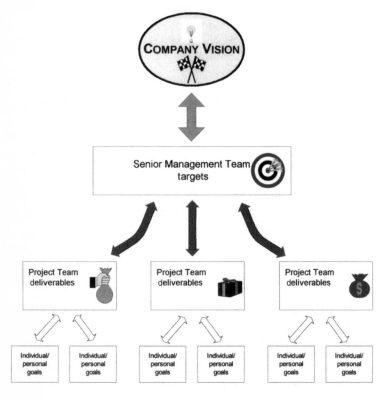

Fig. 12.   Team goals.

These roles may be far from the person's daily job title, but defining the team roles will not only provide you with a balanced team with shared responsibilities, but will also allow team members to know their responsibilities and defined tasks, and have clear identities. You could even draw up job descriptions for these new roles and give them to the team. It also demonstrates that you have a clear idea of the skills needed to complete the project.

ENSURING TEAM FEEDBACK

Teams need to incorporate feedback into their planned work schedules. Feedback is essential so that they can grow together as a team and become more effective. If a team is not performing well, feedback is essential and if team members can learn to both give and receive feedback effectively and without blame, the team can self-improve.

Good feedback techniques

Whether feeding back positive or negative messages, good feedback is:

- specific – it needs to be very clear and should describe a person's behaviour
- immediate – feedback should be given as close to the event as possible for it to be successfully acknowledged and acted on
- within the bounds of action – the resulting action from the feedback needs to be within the bounds of the person's ability or jurisdiction.

Poor feedback techniques

Feedback should never:

- contain too many messages – it will confuse the listener
- be overtly negative – nothing is ever wholly bad, a balance needs to be expressed
- contain personal slights – it is the behaviour you are feeding back on, not the person.

Giving difficult feedback

Giving difficult feedback is never easy but the anxiety can be lessened by:

- finding a private room – never criticise your colleague in front of others

- allowing plenty of time – do not hurry the process

- ending the meeting on a positive note – never leave the meeting without setting out a plan of action or agreeing some targets to aim for.

MAINTAINING A TASK ORIENTATION

The most effective teams achieve a high level of both team and personal goals. The right balance of these two will ensure that everyone is working together as well as achieving for themselves.

However, from time to time teams can lose track of the task they have been assigned. This could be because:

- the team is not being managed properly

- there are too many other (outside team) tasks to be achieved

- team members are being side-tracked by a difficult team member.

In team management, as in project management, you need to maintain a task orientation. You will only achieve the end result by completing a number of tasks or deliverables. Ensure your team maintains this orientation by setting a series of manageable, reasonable and achieveable targets with timescales – even if these are not featured in your project plan.

By setting targets you:

- will ensure that the project moves forward

- can measure your progress

- can celebrate the achievement of each target – which is highly motivating.

Working with project plans

Project planning is a distinct skill whereby stages in a project are mapped out. Each stage of the project journey has a start and end date, and if the stage is a long one it may have several intermediate targets. This plan can be shown in a diagrammatic form and enables the team and all the project stakeholders to track progress. Not all projects need full project planning but by mapping your individual projects by showing their targets on time lines you will be able to see where your project targets are located and if they clash (like trying to achieve too many targets in one month). Project planning software can now easily be bought for installation on your computer. This will enable you to enter each project in turn with milestones or targets, and then print out a 'report' or visual representation of the project which is not only useful for planning but also helpful when trying to explain your project's progress to a third party or to your team.

CELEBRATING TEAM SUCCESS

Always take time out to celebrate success. Teams are working to deadlines and with all the pressure of meeting targets and achieving objectives, small successes can easily be lost. Teams without praise will wither and die. Sometimes the ending will seem so far into the future that the team will lose sight of its objectives; and no one seems to recognise the good work they have done on the way. Set smaller targets and milestones within the team and celebrate reaching them.

As a manager involve others in your celebrations too. Not only are you bringing the project's successes to the attention of others but you are also then raising its profile. The long-term result is that when you next want to pull a team together to deal with a problem or achieve an outcome, you will have people falling over themselves to be on your team. Team work is now being recognised as the way forward in business, and therefore team management is being seen as a positive skill to possess. Good team management includes motivating and celebrating success with your team – not easy but the rewards speak for themselves.

Logging the team journey

If you are working on a long project (of over a year) it can be helpful to log the progress of the team. This is very much like a diary and can be simply made up of monthly notes diarising what the team has learnt during that period. At the end of the project the diary will show not only the project's progress but that of the team too – something you need to discuss in the final team meeting. The advantages are not only for the team, any major points can be fed back to through the organisation to reduce 'reinventing the wheel' at some later date, although it is fascinating to see just how far your have all progressed as individuals.

CASE STUDIES

Tim lays a trap

Tim briefs Alison on what he is going to do. The next day he leaves the two library books prominently on his desk for Pete to see. When Alison comes in to work her shift she comments loudly on the books and ask who they are for. Tim announces assertively that he needs to read the book to help him handle Pete. Pete looks up in amazement and defies anyone to call him 'difficult'. Tim has prepared his speech well and in a calm and level voice explains his issues with Pete. Alison acts as support to his approach and ask both parties if they would try again, emphasising to Pete that they could build a much stronger team if they all worked together. Both Alison and Tim leave Pete a dignified way out of the situation, not blaming the past but promoting the future.

Christine has a shock

Christine is called into the office of her line manager, Trevor Sharp. Trevor tells her that Synchron Software have pulled out of the project, but that he wanted Speedy Software to continue, bringing in the new product alone. Christine is not sure how to tell the team; in one sense Synchron are pulling out after all their hard work and to make matters worse, they will all have to work a lot harder to bring in the project alone. Christine decides to be totally open but upbeat and as part of the recognition of the extra work involved she negotiates a higher completion bonus for the team with Trevor. After all, as they will no longer be paying out to Synchron, they should be able to re-route the money internally to the project team. Christine is nervous about telling the team about Synchron pulling out and the extra work involved, even with their financial reward. However, she is surprised by the unanimous response to taking the project forward alone. However, the team stipulates one condition – that she remains as project manager. Christine is delighted and immediately involves them in her next planning phase.

Jean decides on an approach

Jean decides on a two pronged approach. She cannot expect her manager to shield her from her team and therefore she aims to face her manager with her development need, and deal with her colleagues separately. Jean waits until her manager is out of the office and then asks everyone if they have a few minutes to spare. When they come together, Jean faces them with the fact that she overheard them speaking about her. She tells them that, while their views are their own, she would like to take the opportunity to state her own views. Jean sets out her intentions very seriously and neither becomes emotional nor apportions blame. She tells the small group that she wants to be part of their team and share in the workload. None of the others speaks as they are too embarrassed. Jean finishes the meeting promptly and encourages a return to work.

ACTION POINTS

1. Make a list of the different types of teams you have been involved in.

2. Check that the team (and you) are getting the feedback you deserve.

3. When was the last time you celebrated success? Put a note in your diary to celebrate even the smallest success.

10

Pulling It all Together

Reading a book is very different from taking action. Taking action is testing and puts all you have learnt into perspective. Pull everything together that you have learnt in this book and make a point of never being coerced or bullied by difficult people or caught out by an awkward situation ever again.

ACCEPTING DIFFICULT PEOPLE

Difficult people and awkward situations are everywhere, at work, in social circles and even in the home. Therefore running away is not really an option unless you want to live like a hermit for the remainder of your days.

A far better strategy is to learn to deal with personality difficulties and mismatches. This does not mean being weak, becoming a 'Yes' person, or letting everyone take advantage of you. It means having some firm strategies for dealing with people and situations in your 'tool box', including the strategies you have found in this book.

Consider the advantages of gaining the tools below, and contrast them with the disadvantages of not bothering:

Advantages	Disadvantages
The ability to work with all people.	Being restricted as to whom you can work with.
Being known as a 'people person' who can get things done.	Being seen as weak and ineffectual and being given a wide berth (especially in times of promotion).
Being seen as flexible and someone who can 'deliver', whether that be projects or products.	Being thought difficult yourself owing to your inability to work effectively with others.

LEARNING TO COPE WITH DIFFICULT PEOPLE AT WORK

Think for a minute. Where do you encounter difficult people most? You probably think this is at work, and in that you would not be alone. It is at work that we find all the factors that we do not always find anywhere else: vying for power, financial reward, protection of territory, empire building, complex relations, and I am sure you can think of others.

If you are going to be with someone over a long period of time then you may decide to be open about the difficulties you may face together. It is not always necessary, or even desirable, for people to change their personalities completely before you can work with them. You can achieve a responsible and effective working relationship which gets the task done, based on a short-term agreement between you that any difficult behaviour will only hamper progress.

Naturally this could not go on indefinitely but, on a short-term project or while you are sorting out your next position, it can be a sensible way forward. Always remember that difficult people at work are not fixed in your life, and you can choose to walk away from them and find another job. Ultimately their behaviour is not *your* problem. It is *their* problem, and that of the organisation which has to deal with it.

RECOGNISING DIFFICULT PEOPLE OUTSIDE WORK

Difficult people are not just abundant within organisations. They pervade our social and private life too. Consider these two scenarios:

1. How many times have you moved away from a particular queue at a checkout simply because you do not like the behaviour of the checkout assistant (even though that queue is shorter than the one you have joined)?
2. Or perhaps tried to avoid visiting Aunt Maud and Uncle Henry because they bark at you and make you feel as though you have done something wrong?

The checkout assistant situation is easy because you can just choose to avoid it – you simply go to another checkout. But it is a bit foolish, especially if the queue really is longer at the other counter. In this situation avoidance is quite a good strategy because you cannot engage with the person long enough to hope to effect any change in their behaviour. If you really wanted to do that you would have to speak with the assistant's manager, so that they could see whether it was an isolated incident or whether the behaviour problem was persistent.

The relation situation is more complex. Old Aunt Maud and Uncle Henry are part of your past and, in that, are part of you. Personal and family relationships are complex and have much more at stake. In falling out with one member of your family, you can set off a whole chain of repercussions which can effectively split a family apart. This does not mean to say that you have to put up with uncomfortable or difficult behaviour, it just means that you need to think more carefully about how you will approach things and take into consideration a large number of factors and repercussions. Cutting relatives out of your life is not usually the best way forward and you may have to consider other coping techniques such as reducing the number of times you see them, or writing rather than visiting (for one-way, controlled communication).

RE-VISITING THE TECHNIQUES

If you regularly look over some of the techniques found in this book, you will have to hand a complete 'tool kit' for dealing with the difficult people you meet.

Many of the techniques require you to practise before putting them into operation, and they may not feel comfortable at first. It can be quite frightening to confront someone about their behaviour, especially if they have been acting this way for many years and you have been allowing them to get away with it. The secret here is to stay firm. Once you have decided to take action, see it through. Teachers will tell you that if they let a child get away with poor behaviour or answering back, the child will do it again. Poor behaviour needs to be dealt with firmly and in a responsible manner.

If you find approaching the person in the first place too much to handle, you may find a book on assertive techniques quite helpful. Assertiveness teaches you about taking forward decisive action about your own feelings, and again there are helpful techniques you can use. A mentoring relationship may also offer helpful support, especially over a long period of time.

Never feel lost and alone, there is always help at hand and no situation is ever irredeemable even if the bottom line is mutual avoidance or deciding to leave your job. It is so easy to blame oneself but even if you have not managed the situation as well as your could, dwelling on this will be defeatist and achieve nothing. The ability to remember, reason about, and learn from the past is a particular human skill. Therefore it is good to dwell on the happy memories and bask in the warmth they give. In contrast, you must not dwell on the bad memories, rather you must learn from them. Make it your intention now to always move onwards, never stagnating in the past.

THINKING OVER YOUR OWN BEHAVIOUR

Although many of the techniques are offered here as remedies for the poor behaviour of others, you need to always think of your own behaviour before acting. Ask yourself honestly:

'Did I incite that response?' and

'Was there anything I could have done differently to have effected a different outcome?'

If the answer to both of these is 'No' then you may proceed. However, if the answer is 'Yes' then you need to ask yourself whether it is fair to check someone for a behaviour which is encouraged by yourself. For example if you create a culture of competition in your office, you cannot be surprised when someone tries to outdo you by whatever means it takes. Their behaviour may be poor but could you really say that you had no hand in fostering it?

One area where self-reflection of behaviour is vital when an individual is the victim of sexual harassment. Behavioural reflection is important because one of the ploys often used by those harassing others is to claim that they incited this response, leading them on. You must stand firm on this. By all means think through your previous behaviour, but do not be hard on yourself. Light joking banter, even if it slightly flirtatious, does not invite others to harass you sexually.

RESPECTING OTHERS

We are all different. We come from different cultures and have different backgrounds. Often those very differences make us fight each other and create barriers. How much easier it is to thrive on those differences.

Next time you are introducing a team worker or colleague who has very different views from your own, do not say, 'This is Jane. We can't agree on anything, can we Jane?' Instead introduce her as, 'This is Jane. She is really valuable to our team as she has an interesting and diverse set of views that always gets me thinking'. The more you use this type of language, the more you will actually believe it and it will have a very noticeable effect on your colleagues like Jane. They will acknowledge that you do not see their behaviour as threatening, and can, in fact, manage it very well. You will never rise in stature by putting other people down.

Sometimes the very language we habitually use can help us to respect the views and comments of others. Before spouting a new idea as 'Ridiculous, absolutely absurd!' try saying, 'That's interesting, tell me more about that' – it may be that when explained more fully the idea is not absurd at all and may have many good points. In fact the word 'interesting', depending on how it is said, can hold several different connotations and cover many an embarrassing moment. Find your own, carefully chosen expressions and start using them regularly – you will soon find them an easy part of your everyday language.

UNDERSTANDING THE IMPORTANCE OF ANGER AND CONFLICT MANAGEMENT

Anger is a natural feeling especially within a conflict situation. However, management of that anger is essential. This does not mean suppressing the anger so that it causes you internal stress. Neither does it mean leaving the room, only to put your fist through a door or shout at the next person you meet. Anger and conflict management means dealing effectively with your feelings so that they can be expressed clearly without losing control. Being out of control often feels as bad as it looks. Not only does everyone duck for cover, but you also find yourself having to hide from them for the next week while you recover from your embarrassment.

Of course the anger is not always yours. Managing someone else's anger is also a discrete skill. The main points here are:

- try to get them to sit down – pacing will only exacerbate anger

- neither crowd in nor be too distant – keep a distance of at least a metre between you

- try to maintain eye contact with them and use your body language to express that you are listening to them – sit forward and acknowledge their comments

- show empathy not sympathy – try to put yourself in their position and do not be patronising

- keep an even tone to your voice – do not let your voice rise or express frustration.

Finally when their anger has abated, try to move into joint problem solving, always leaving the conversation on a positive note.

GAINING CONFIDENCE

As you practise dealing with difficult people your confidence will grow. Each time you deal with a difficult situation, life in general will become a little easier as it will no longer hold the same fears for you. You will not fear the people and situations that haunt and hold back so many others, and may even feel the need to surge ahead in your own career.

People management is gaining prominence as a skill to be acknowledged. Businesses of the future need staff who can communicate effectively and have the ability to get people to do the job or complete the task. Being proficient in these skills will enable you to shine, stand head and shoulders above others, and get you noticed for promotion.

Look around you and you will see that the people at the top are the people who achieve results. More and more these results can only be achieved through good people management. It is still possible to bully people into doing what you want, but everyone knows how you have reached that goal. You would soon find out that people will not want to work with you. In fact people do not even want to associate with a bully and on many occasions you would stand alone – and it can be very lonely out there. How much more comfortable to take your team and colleagues with you, all the way up. Let them share in your success and feel included. Not only will they help you to achieve success but also help you to repeat the recipe over and over again. People management is a great skill and dealing with difficult people is part of that skill. Work on your own methods and techniques, injected with your natural personality, and watch it pay dividends in terms not only of your confidence but also your career.

Using open learning
Embarking on a programme of learning has been proven as a way of gaining or increasing confidence, particularly in communication and personal skills. Even if you find it difficult to access training or support through your work, you could embark on a programme of open learning through either your local library (which is able to obtain a selection of programmes), or through a course provider such as a college. Even if you cannot locate a programme which deals with managing difficult people, simply undertaking a course will help your confidence to grow and you could enhance some of the associated skills mentioned such as assertiveness, people management, problem solving and others.

CASE STUDIES

Tim shares his secret
Bob Green asks Tim in again to see how things are going. He comments that the whole atmosphere has changed and that the number of effectively handled calls has increased by 20 per cent. Tim explains how the books provided the necessary prompt to get everyone talking, and Bob is impressed. He makes a note in Tim's personal file that if he is able to take on behavioural problems like Pete's then he will go far.

Christine gets an offer
Sue contacts Christine to tell her that an early place has come up on the managing difficult people programme, and would she like to take it? This sets Christine thinking. She no longer sees her team as difficult people, just as people, nor feels the urgent need to seek outside advice. Christine reflects that she has relaxed, the project is going well (even if it is still a little behind schedule). The last few weeks have not been easy, but with good sense she has managed to come through. She decides that she will go on the

course but because she does not need it so urgently she sticks to her original timescale, thereby letting someone else take the last minute vacancy. Trevor has noticed how much more effectively the team is working and offers Christine the job of project manager on a permanent basis.

Jean gets what she wants
Jean says nothing of her confrontation with the team to her manager at their next monthly meeting. However, she outlines the actions which have not been completed since their last meeting, and while not stating any reason or blaming anyone, has a list of effects this has had – for example, the computer inputting is now even further behind. Finally Jean offers her manager a way forward. She suggests that, although Janie is the computer expert in the team, she is also very busy. Perhaps it would be better if Susan were to introduce her to the system, and then she can become more proficient in the more complex operations when Janie has more time. Jean's manager thinks this is an excellent way forward and calls Susan in to discuss it. At last it looks as though Jean will get her training.

ACTION POINTS

1. Think of three things that you could do now to make you feel more confident about your ability to tackle the next difficult person or situation which comes along.

2. Can you think of a time when you snapped at a colleague only to be snapped back at? How did that make you feel?

3. Make a list of all the people you have difficult working relationships with, then write one thing you like about them beside each name. Try at some point in the future to compliment them on that one thing – it will build bridges for the future.

Glossary

360° feedback. A tool for assessing development needs.

Action learning set. A group of people meeting to learn from each other and share experiences.

Appraisal. An assessment of someone's work performance.

Assertiveness. A technique of confident and direct behaviour.

Autonomy. Self-governing.

Away days. Days out of the working environment to allow social activity and learning.

Body language. Non-verbal communication.

Broken record. A technique of verbal repetition often used in the training of assertiveness.

Bullying. Hurting, persecuting or intimidating others.

Channels of communication. Different ways of communication.

Colour therapy. The use of colours to impact on moods and/or behaviour.

Congruent. Corresponding or agreeing.

Consultant. A specialist who gives expert advice.

Cultural barriers. The ideas, beliefs, values and knowledge surrounding one group of people, which hinder the interface with another group.

Customer loyalty. Customers preferring your products to any other.

Customer power. When the customer has a high level of influence on a business.

Empathise. The act of attempting to feel what a situation or emotion may be like for another person.

External customers. Customers outside of the organisation or company, *eg* other businesses.

Feedback. Providing constructive comments on performance following an event or action.

Fight or flight. Increased energy to resolve conflict by either fighting or running away.

Geographical differences. Differences founded on people coming from different locations.

Hecklers. People who shout down presenters or performers.

Internal customers. Customers within the organisation or company, *eg* different departments.

Jargon. Short-form language used by specialist groups.

Learning curve. A geographical representation of learning. A curve travelling upwards.

Log. A written record similar to a diary.

Mediation. An attempt to reconcile disputes.

Mentor. A wise person.

Monitoring mechanisms. A way of measuring progress.

Non-verbal. Not spoken.

Paraphrase. To replay the meaning of a conversation or piece of text, using other words.

Patronise. To treat in a condescending way.

Plan of action. A structured set of related items which describe the options for taking learning forward to meet specified goals.

Problem solving group. A group of people brought together to try and jointly solve problems.

Procrastinate. To put off or defer.

Protagonist. A principal character.

Self-esteem. A favourable opinion of yourself.

Skills development. Developing expert and practised abilities.

Team building. Methods to enable team members to work more effectively together.

Tool box. A box of useful instruments – skills, in a management context.

Victimisation. To punish or discriminate against.

Win:win. A solution whereby both parties win.

Further Reading

30 Minutes to Deal with Difficult People, Cary L Cooper and Valerie Sutherland (Kogan Page).

Dealing with Difficult People, Roberta Cava (Piatkus Books).

How to Cope with Difficult People, Alan Houel (Sheldon Press).

How to Deal with Difficult People, Ursula Markham (Thorsons).

How to Deal with People You Can't Stand, Rick Brinkman (McGraw).

Assertiveness at Work (A Practical Guide to Handling Awkward Situations), Ken and Kate Back (BIBLIOS).

Developing Assertiveness – Self-Development for Managers, Anni Townend (ITPS).

Assertiveness for Managers, Terry Gillen (Gower Publishing).

Successful Mentoring in a Week – Successful Business in a Week, Gareth Lewis and Stephen Caster (Headway).

The Manager as Coach and Mentor – Management Shapers, Eric Parsloe (Institute of Personnel and Development).

Mentoring (A Guide to the Basics) – Better Management Skills, Gordon F Shea (Kogan Page).

The Business of Listening, Diane Bone (Crisp Publications).

Teams, Teamwork and Teambuilding, Kenneth Stott and Allan Walker (Prentice Hall).

Useful Addresses

INSTITUTES AND BUSINESS HELP

Institute of Management, Management House, Cottingham Road, Corby, Northants NN17 1TT. Tel: (01536) 204222. www.inst-mgt.org.uk

Chartered Institute of Personnel Development, CIPD House, Camp Road, London SW19 4UX. Tel: (020) 8971 9000. www.cipd.co.uk

Chartered Institute of Marketing, Moor Hall, Cookham, Maidenhead, Berks SL6 9QH. Tel: (01628) 427500. www.cim.co.uk

Institute for the Management of Information Systems, IMIS, 5 Kingfisher House, New Mill Road, Orpington, Kent BR5 3QG. Tel: (0700) 002 3456. www.imis.org.uk

Institute of Sales and Marketing Management, Romeland House, Romeland Hill, St Albans, Herts AL3 4ET. Tel: (01727) 812500. www.ismm.co.uk

Learning Skills Directorates, see your local *Yellow Pages*.

Department of Trade and Industry (DTI), DTI publications Orderline, Admail 528, London SW1W 8YT. Tel: (0870) 1502 500. www.dti.gov.uk

The Industrial Society, Peter Runge House, 3 Carlton House, Terrace, London SW1Y 5DG. Tel: (0870) 400 1000. www.indsoc.co.uk

Equal Opportunities Commission, Arndale House, Arndale Centre, Manchester M4 3EQ. Tel: (0161) 833 9244. www.eoc.org.uk

TRAINING

Local colleges, see your local *Yellow Pages*.

Qualifications in Curriculum Authority (*NVQ information*), 89 Piccadilly, London W1J 8AQ. Tel: (020) 7509 5555. www.qca.org.uk

Adult Education, see your local *Yellow Pages*.

TRAINING (OPEN LEARNING)

Open and Distance Learning Quality Council, 16 Park Crescent, London W1B 1AH. Tel: (020) 7612 7090. www.odlqc.org.uk

The Open University, PO Box 71, Milton Keynes MK1 6AG. Tel: (01908) 274066. www.open.ac.uk

Index

£8.99.